HARSH REALITY

Tales of the Z-List from a Reality Star Booking Agent

HARSH

REALITY

TALES OF THE Z-LIST FROM A REALITY STAR BOOKING AGENT

Andy Binder

BLUE RIVER PRESS

Harsh Reality: Tales of The Z-list From a Reality Star Booking Agent
Copyright © 2018 by Andy Binder

Published by Blue River Press
Indianapolis, Indiana
www.brpressbooks.com

Distributed by Cardinal Publishers Group
A Tom Doherty Company, Inc.
www.cardinalpub.com

ISBN: 978-1-68157-073-0

Cover Design: Lee Dixon
Cover Photograph: Ceara Poulin
Book Design: Glen M. Edelstein
Editor: Dani McCormick
Photographs: Courtesy of the Author

The author has tried to recreate events, locales, and conversations from his memory of them. In order to maintain their anonymity, in some instances names of individuals and places have been changed. Identifying characteristics, features, and details may also have been changed.

Printed in the United States of America

22 21 20 19 18   1 2 3 4 5

The book is dedicated to all of the reality star fans out there who've ever came to, or will come to, one of our crazy appearances

CONTENTS

HARSH REALITY

Tales of the Z-List from a Reality Star Booking Agent

PROLOGUE

2015. BOSTON, MA

"ANDY!" MIKE SHOUTS FROM THE DRESSING room, "We'll be ready in ten minutes!"

Good. Don't want to keep the ladies waiting.

I peek out from the side of the stage to check out the audience. Every seat is filled, and the crowd of over a thousand females is just pulsating with energy and excitement, waiting for the guys to take the stage. This show was sold out weeks ago, and there are no last minute tickets available anywhere.

Everything is going great. Our guaranteed payment is already higher than it's ever been, and with the sold-out crowd we'll be getting a huge bonus on the back end. It still feels surreal to me that I'm standing here, a booking agent for an act that's been performing to sold-out crowds across the United States.

The act is called *Men of the Strip*; it's a male revue based out of Las Vegas, and it was formed by Jeff Timmons of 98 Degrees. The revue has just been featured on a two-hour movie special on the *E!* Network. They're hot, they're happening, and I'm their booking agent. Pretty damn cool.

Mike, their manager and co-owner, likes to keep me on my toes.

"Andy, how we doing?" he yells from down the hall, and I know it's time to make the final rounds and see that everything is in place and ready for show time. Spinning away from the stage, I almost trip on an electrical cord as I start running around backstage like a madman, making sure all is in order, everyone is happy, nothing is left to chance.

First stop is Jeff's dressing room. Jeff will be hosting the show and also performing some of his 98 Degrees mega-hits as part of the set. He's the Man.

"Jeff, you all good?" I say through the closed door.

"Andy!" I hear him respond from inside. "How many times have I told you, get the fuck in here and have a drink with me!"

Jeff's that rare thing, a client who's becoming more and more like a good friend. He isn't the kind of celebrity who doesn't want you hanging out in his dressing room. On the contrary, he gets annoyed if you try to kiss his ass.

So I head into the dressing room, and there's Jeff just chilling on the couch, holding his drink in one hand, and a second one out to me in the other.

"Come on, Andy, have a beer with me before I hit the stage."

"Well—just one. I gotta be professional."

Jeff laughs, and rags on me: "Yeah, right. *You*, professional!"

"No, seriously. We're getting paid a shitload of money to be here, and I'm working right now." And I *am* serious. It's important to me—when around professionals, I present myself like a professional. 'Cause it wasn't always this way. I paid my dues with a lot of amateurs to get to this point, and I have no intention of going backwards. "I'll do shots at the after party. But right now it's down to business."

"Okay, you don't have to give me a speech. Just drink the fucking beer," Jeff jokes.

So I drink the fucking beer.

After which I run out of his dressing room and over to the sound board to make sure they have everything they need. Time to cue up the louder music and really hype the anticipation of the crowd. The theater starts to sound like a loud rocking nightclub, and the audience begins to dance. Now they're chanting, "Men of the Strip! Men of the Strip!" It's a beautiful sound.

At that exact moment my phone starts vibrating in my pocket. Who is calling me now...?

Ah shit, it's the girls I met last time I had an event in Boston. They texted me last week asking if I could put them on the VIP guest list for tonight. Sure, I said. And then promptly forgot.

This could be bad.

I run up to the venue lobby and they're standing there, arms folded, eyes glaring, teeth bared, looking hot but pissed.

"Ladies, ladies...!" I say jocularly, trying to defuse their anger. "You look amazing!"

"Andy," says the leader of the pack, "what the hell, we're not on the list!"

"The list...?" I feign ignorance.

"The VIP list!"

"Oh—really?" I walk over to the will call window and study the list carefully, as if expecting to find their names hidden somewhere in the margins. "That's not right."

The Leader isn't buying my confusion. "You promised you'd take care of us!" she snarls.

I decide to drop the bewildered act and come clean, save myself a lot of bullshit. "You know, I got so busy backstage with the guys dealing with stuff, I must have forgot, and the show's totally sold out, there's no seats left at all."

All those pretty mascaraed eyes widen with outrage. "So we can't even get in?"

I can see the girls are about to explode, and it's not going to be pretty, so it's time to play my trusty ace in the hole.

"Look, we have no spare seats, but I'll walk you in. I'll give you extra passes so you can watch the show from the side of the stage."

"From the stage?" Now those same pretty eyes all light up like diamonds. "Ohh fuck yeah!"

I figured that would turn the tide. People always love the idea of watching from the wings. It's the same show, but they think they're seeing something special. VIP style.

"I knew you'd come through for us, Andy. We're all gonna party after the show, right?"

"Of course," I say, "I'm looking forward to it." Especially now.

I flash my backstage pass to the security guys at the door, tell them the girls are with me, and he waves us all in. It's only two minutes to show time so I make the girls follow me fast as I run down the aisle to the side stage entrance.

"Hang out over here, best view in the house. Enjoy the show and I'll text you after."

"Awesome! Thanks Andy, you're the best!"

"I know," I yell back, as I'm already halfway down the back-stage hall.

Now the sound engineer hands me the wireless mic for Jeff as I run past him. It's perfect timing since five seconds later I see Jeff walking out of his dressing room.

"Here's your mic, Jeff. You ready?"

"Always ready," Jeff says confidently.

Not so fast. While we're standing there, Mike runs over. He looks alarmed. Not a good sign when the manager is alarmed.

"Andy, we got a problem. Half the guys are refusing to go on stage."

"What?" I knew this was going way too smoothly.

"They say a lot of the food and drinks they requested in the contract rider weren't in the dressing room, so they're pissed and they don't wanna perform."

"Are you fucking kidding me?" The shock is clear on my face.

Mike gives a helpless shrug, and then breaks into a grin. "Yes I'm kidding, dude. When are you gonna learn that I just love fucking with you?"

Yeah, I should've known.

"Ha ha, you're right, asshole. Can you get the guys to stage left? We need them on in thirty seconds, Jeff's about to go on."

"On it! They're coming down now. Costumes on and ready," Mike replies.

Showtime! I head over to the light guy and tell him to turn off the house lights, get the spotlight on, and crank up the intro music. At that moment, the sheer loudness of the crowd blows me away. All of the excitement and anticipation for the show to start, building, building, building, and now it's finally here. The place is louder than a Justin Bieber concert. And it should be, because these ladies are in for the show of their lives. Jeff Timmons and the *Men of the Strip* never disappoint.

And as Jeff walks on stage, and the crowd goes wild, the electric rush of the moment hits me, and I think about how I got here. It sure as hell wasn't always like this. The journey was crazy, insane, and unreal. But if it weren't for the past decade or so, I never would have made it to this point. I never would have reached this pinnacle.

CHAPTER 1
THE INSANITY BEGINS

I LOVE THE ENTERTAINMENT BUSINESS. ALWAYS have. Since I was a kid. All of it—the performers, the music, the glitz and the glamour, the backstage intrigue. . . . The thrill of the show-biz world has always excited the hell out of me.

And when I went to my first live concert, it sealed the deal. The sheer visceral intensity of the music, the hysteria of the crowd, the wave upon wave of sensory overload—it was exhilarating, and totally addictive.

But it wasn't enough to be an audience member—I wanted to be a part of that world. I wanted inside. How could I not? It was in my DNA, it was meant to be. Some way, somehow, somewhere.

Somewhere turned out to be the State University of New York at Geneseo. It was a typical state college—good faculty, decent education system, lots of partying. I had no big career plans at the time; I went to college because everybody else did. But soon enough I had the opportunity to join the university's student events board. One of the duties of the board was to schedule and organize big concerts on campus, and bring in name performers. Was I interested? I jumped at it.

My first backstage concert experience was as a freshman. I'll never forget it. Matchbox Twenty. One of the top pop/rock bands in the country at the time. The concert committee on the events board brought them to campus, and I volunteered for every single shift the entire day. My hope was that I would get the chance to meet them. Who knew what would happen from there?

On the day of the concert I arrived at 8 am to help set up the dressing room. College concerts are often in the campus gymnasium, and dressing rooms are usually spruced-up athletic department offices. But we did everything we could to make it seem like the dressing room of a high-end stadium venue. That was something I grasped early on: take care of the Talent, because without them there's no show. It was a busy day of non-stop preparation, getting everything ready. The band was doing a sound check at 5 pm, and I was looking forward to helping them out and making sure all went smoothly: "You need coffee? No problem. You want it quiet? I'm on it!"

I really wanted them to be totally impressed with me: "Hey, who's that kid? He really belongs in this business!"

It was just before five, as we waited for the band to come down, when the president of the concert committee approached us.

"They're doing a closed sound check," he said. "You guys need to wait in the main lobby."

Kicked out. Disappointing. But being the obedient freshman that I was—if I'd been a little older I would have figured out a way to finagle myself in—I exited backstage and consoled myself with the thought that the big concert itself was just a few hours away.

And when those lights in the gym went out and the sold-out crowd of 3,000 fellow students started cheering, I was hooked. All the hard work of the day was about to pay off with an incredible show.

And incredible it was. The performance, energy and crowd interaction of Matchbox Twenty was, pardon the pun, unmatched.

And the day's hard work really paid off when, at the end of the show, the tour manager told us that the band was so impressed with our hosting, and so happy with the way the show turned out, that they wanted to do a special meet-and-greet for all of the student volunteers who helped make it happen.

So it was that about thirty minutes after the show ended and the crowd was gone, me and my fellow committee friends were hanging out in the bleachers, anxiously awaiting the group's appearance. All of a sudden they were there—Matchbox Twenty—and of course I was the first one to head over to Rob Thomas, the lead singer.

"Mr. Thomas, your show was amazing! Thank you so much for coming to Geneseo," I said, trying not to stutter.

He gave me a wry smile. "Dude, Mr. Thomas is my dad. Call me Rob!"

He was such a cool guy, still one of the nicest celebrities I've ever met. Rob ended up hanging out with out all of us for a while after the show

It was truly that experience that set me on the path to come. It wasn't just the concert itself, but hanging with the band afterwards, that convinced me that I was born for this kind of life. Screw Business Management, or Teaching, or Political Science; I wanted to major in Concert Management.

I threw myself heart and soul into the task of programming concert events for Geneseo, and my dedication was rewarded the following year when, as a sophomore, I was elected president and chair of the Geneseo Concerts Committee branch of the student events board. And subsequently re-elected my junior and senior years. My role was to bring in big name concerts twice a year for the campus community. I was looking for acts that would appeal to a wide range of students, acts that were well-known and on their way to becoming even bigger. And I made some good bookings throughout my years as concert chair at Geneseo. There were sold-out shows for 3 Doors Down and Nelly, and I even booked a show where Black Eyed Peas was the opening act, before it went on to become a superstar band. I also booked a couple of duds, who were big at the moment but whose stardom didn't last.

My experience booking and producing major concerts was more fun and more educational than any college class I could take, and it also introduced me to NACA. The National Association of Campus Activities is an organization that brings college student event programmers and their advisors together with agents, artists, bands, singers, speakers and other celebrities who want to perform on the college circuit. Being the head of concerts at Geneseo, I was one of the few student reps from campus who was able to attend the NACA conference each year. It was awesome going to these big conferences and schmoozing with agents and celebrities who, in turn, were trying to schmooze me so I'd book them at my college. A simple show-biz fact: it's all about the circle of schmoozing.

After college graduation, the high I'd been riding from my little taste of the entertainment world started to wear off, and heading back home to Albany, NY. I had to start focusing on what I really wanted to do next. As it turned out, my old friend Mayo shared a similar passion for the entertainment business. One day we were out pursuing our usual routine, getting beers at our favorite Albany bar.

About four beers deep, I laid it all out for Mayo. "I really wanna be an agent, and book concerts and events and celebrities."

Mayo nodded. "Yeah, me too."

"So why don't we start a business together and do it?"

"I'm down with that," Mayo said. "But how? We can't just say we're agents. We gotta have contacts."

I'd already thought about this: "When I was at Geneseo I used to go to this conference called NACA, and agents were there meeting people, networking, getting clients, booking shows. I think we should reserve a booth this year. As agents. We'll get all the contacts we need."

As I explained the workings of NACA in detail, Mayo got hooked on the idea.

"My dad is a lawyer," he said, getting excited. "I can get him to do all the paperwork and register us as an LLC. We'll be good to go in no time."

"Awesome! It's a plan!" On to the fifth beer.

When we sobered up the next day, we decided to stick with our drunken idea. I got a friend to set up a website for us, Mayo's dad registered us as a business, and we split the cost to sign up for a booth at NACA. This was in the late summer of 2003, and the conference was in October in Baltimore, so that gave us a good two months to organize and plan.

Only we didn't. Oh, we were smart enough to get banners and handouts with our business info included, but that was about it. We advertised ourselves as booking agents for concerts, comedians, and speakers. But we didn't have a roster of anyone. No clients whatsoever.

Still, we showed up at NACA hoping for the best. We were enthusiastic, we were driven, and we figured our sheer desire to succeed would trump any lack of professional slickness.

Our hopes started to sink immediately when we looked around at the booth displays in the exhibit hall. The agencies and bands all had flashy top-of-the-line set-ups with electronics, lights, TVs, fancy giveaways, and more. We had a black-and-white banner and paper flyers.

I looked at Mayo. "I think we're fucked," I said.

"I think you're right."

Nevertheless, we put on our game faces and stuck it out as the exhibit hall opened and everyone started pouring in. There were college student event leaders, college staff event programmers, and of course hundreds of agents, managers, and various celebrities.

But while there was a fair share of big names, we started to notice something else: there were also plenty of low-level celebrities and stars past their prime. Singers who were one-hit wonders ten years ago, hoping to get back on the college circuit. Comedians who had a big role in one movie fifteen years ago, still trying to make a living riding on that fame.

And then, another group of people I didn't expect to see at all, a type of alternate celebrity who could be found in almost every corner of the exhibit hall. Reality Stars.

Reality stars were all over the place. Not former reality stars, but current members of ongoing shows. It seemed NACA was their next stop once the season stopped filming. There were stars there from every major reality show at the time: *The Apprentice, Survivor, Real World,* and *Real World/Road Rules Challenge* (now known simply as *The Challenge*).

As we were gawking in amazement at all the random celebrities in the exhibit hall, most of whom passed by our modest little booth with barely a glance, I turned to my right and spotted this gorgeous girl, tan with long brown hair and an air of confidence in her step, heading our way. I figured this vision of beauty was on an urgent mission somewhere and was going to move right past us, but no, she came right up to the booth, face to face with us.

"Hey. I'm Veronica."

No shit. Of course she was Veronica, she didn't have to tell me or Mayo or anybody else in the hall that. Veronica Portillo, hottest star of MTV's *Road Rules Semester at Sea* and several seasons of *The Real World/Road Rules Challenge*, and a featured celebrity model in a recent issue of *Playboy*—Veronica Portillo was introducing herself to *us*. But why?

"What do you guys do?"

I was speechless for a few seconds. Finally I put out my hand to shake hers.

"Hi Veronica, I'm Andy, and this is Mayo." Okay, what else? "We're both big fans."

She gave a glance at our banner, and waited for me to say something more professionally enlightening. I could see that the window of opportunity was going to close as soon as it had opened if I didn't get my shit together fast.

"So—We just started a new business, booking entertainment, and we came here to make some connections, do some networking."

Veronica nodded. "Nice. Yeah, Rachel and I are also here to network."

Rachel—it took me a millisecond to register that Rachel was Rachel Robinson, another hot reality star from *Road Rules*. She was here, too?

"We're looking for agents to represent us and get us paid for events."

Boom! The conversation went from being exciting to life-changing in thirty seconds. I wasn't star-struck anymore, I was sensing a golden opportunity. They were looking for agents, we were looking for clients. No sense in playing coy—go for it.

"You came to the right place." I declared, with the same confidence that Veronica was pushing. "We're your guys."

Veronica smiled at my boldness. "Really?"

"We're new to this business but we're hungry, we're hard-working, and we're ready to make you some money. Right, Mayo?"

"Right," said Mayo, playing the near-silent partner.

I decided to go for the full-court press. "Speaking of hungry, how about we take you and Rachel out to dinner later and discuss how we can work together?"

She didn't blink. "Sounds like a plan to me."

So Veronica gave me her number and told me to call in a few hours after the exhibit hall closed, so we could finalize our dinner plans. Yes, she actually told me to call her (remember, this was 2003, and texting was a lot rarer back then). And now I had Veronica Portillo's number. I couldn't believe it.

Andy with Veronica and Rachel at the exhibit hall booth at NACA

Mayo and I schmoozed a few other people during the next few hours at NACA, but nothing seemed promising. Didn't matter: we were excited about our dinner later with Veronica and Rachel, that's all that occupied our minds. After we left the exhibit hall we found a computer and searched for good restaurants in Baltimore. We found a steakhouse that looked great, and within walking distance of the hotel, so we made a reservation. I got in touch with Veronica, and it turned out that they were staying in the same hotel as we were. So we said we'd meet in the lobby at 6:45, then walk over for our 7 pm reservation.

The next hour was spent trying, as best we could, to look the part of agents. After my nice high-pressure hotel shower, I got out the ironing board, took out the badly folded clothes from my suitcase, and ironed away. The ensemble was a bright purple horizontal-striped button-down shirt, boot cut jeans, and black dress shoes. That was a hot outfit for 2003, if I do so say myself. I thought I fit the part perfectly.

Mayo, not so much. He had only a t-shirt and corduroys. We finished prepping, did ten sprays of Abercrombie & Fitch cologne each, and headed for the elevator to the lobby.

We got down there right at a quarter to seven, and no surprise, we beat them. Hey, they're girls and they're famous, so we knew they'd be taking their sweet time getting ready. I called the restaurant to let them know we'd probably be a few minutes late, and then sat on a couch in the hotel lobby across from Mayo.

"Dude, can you believe this shit?" I said to him.

"No man, first celebrities we've ever really hung out with. We finally hit the big time."

"Chill, Mayo, one step at a time. Let's remember, they're reality stars. Who knows what we'll even get out of this meeting? Except an expensive-as-hell steakhouse bill that we'll have to pay for."

Mayo nodded. "True. Let's see how it goes. It could be nothing. It could be a waste."

I grinned. "Or it could be fantastic!"

A few minutes later the elevator doors slid open, and two stunning females walked out. Wow. Both dressed in sexy but conservative mode, showing a little skin but not too much. Of course you really can't ever show too much for my tastes, but it was a respectable amount for this first agent/client meeting. Veronica tapped Rachel and pointed in our direction, while we got up and met them halfway.

"Rachel, this is Andy and Mayo," Veronica said.

Mayo stuck out his hand for a handshake. "Great to meet you."

"Likewise," I added. "Ready to head over?"

"Let's do it," Veronica and Rachel responded in unison.

It was mid-October in Baltimore, and while fall was in the air, for us upstate New Yorkers it felt pretty mild. Not so for Veronica and Rachel, who were both from California and used to warmer weather. And who both had a lot more exposed to the elements than we did.

"Walk faster," Veronica said. "I'm freezing my ass off."

We walked briskly into the restaurant a few minutes later, and were greeted by a perky girl at the hostess stand.

"Reservation for four, under Andy," I said to her in my professional, agent-like way.

The hostess was staring at Veronica and Rachel.

"Ohmygod! You're from MTV!" she squealed, hurting all of our ears.

"Yeah, hi, how are you?" Veronica replied.

"Holy shit holy shit holy shit!" the hostess said over and over, her needle stuck in a groove. "I'm a huge fan of *Real World/Road Rules Challenge!* HUGE!"

"So, reservation for four. . . ." I repeated.

She totally ignored me. "Can I pleeeeeease have a picture with you two? Pleeeease?"

"Sure," Rachel answered graciously.

The hostess ran in the back and returned thirty seconds later, camera in hand. Again, it was 2003; no smart phone cameras yet. She handed me the camera, without even acknowledging me, and walked over between Veronica and Rachel to get a photo.

"Sure, I'll be happy to take the picture," I said sarcastically. Which had no effect, she didn't hear me. She was in the zone.

After snapping a few shots, I handed the camera back to her.

"So, can we have our table now?" Mayo asked.

"Oh yeah, sorry. I got kinda star struck. I've never met a celebrity before. I CANNOT believe Veronica and Rachel are here."

Mayo and I looked at each other and rolled our eyes in annoyance, conveniently forgetting that we were just as star-struck a few hours earlier. After a few more gushing accolades from the hostess, we finally made it to the table. Everyone ordered drinks, finalized whatever expensive cuts of steak we wanted to indulge in, put in the meal order and another round of drinks, then got down to business.

"Okay guys," Veronica started. "They keep asking us back for new seasons of the *Real World/Road Rules Challenge*, which is great, but in between filming we'd love to make more money."

"We know the opportunities are there," said Rachel, "but we don't have the time to tap into them."

"That's where you would come in," said Veronica.

"So basically you want us to get you set up on the college circuit?" I asked.

"We want you to set us up *everywhere*," said Veronica. "Colleges, nightclubs, wherever. We can host a contest, do meet-and-greets, anything the bar or nightclub wants us to do. We'll do the work if you get us the gigs."

"We can do that. We know how to sell," I assured her, omitting the fact that we hadn't sold anything yet. "We have a lot of college connections, and we got no problem cold-calling nightclubs across the country, we'll see if they're interested—"

"Oh, they're *going* to be interested," Veronica insisted. "Look, fuck the false modesty—we're both names, we've got followings, we know we'll attract a crowd. If you hype the fact that bringing us in for an appearance will help increase business, they'll definitely go for it."

"How much do you usually get for one of these nightclub appearances?" I asked.

Rachel said. "Anywhere from $1,200 to $2,500, usually."

"And you'll get twenty percent of whatever we get," added Veronica.

Not bad. I could make up to $500 per appearance just by making a few phone calls. From the way Mayo was nodding and smiling, I could tell he was making the same calculation. We were both pretty good at math.

"So, if it's both of you on the same night at the same club, we could ask for $5,000?" I asked, my mind on the fact that that would mean $1,000 in my pocket.

"Yeah of course, we prefer to do events together if possible," Veronica said. "We know that's not always doable for the venue, and we would take less than $5,000, but it's a good starting point for negotiations."

"Absolutely", I agreed.

"What about colleges?" asked Mayo, speaking up for the first time. "What kind of pay is that?"

"Colleges are a gold mine," said Rachel. "They'll pay us $5,000 to $7,500 each. That's why we're at NACA. Trying to get college gigs."

"And since you guys are already members of NACA," said Veronica, "you can follow up with all the contacts you meet at the conference this week."

My mind was spinning with the thought of all that money coming in, but I still had the presence of mind for a nuts-and-bolts question. "What exactly do you do at colleges? That's a whole different venue from nightclubs."

"We give speeches."

"Speeches? About what?" I didn't mean to be insulting, but what did reality stars have to talk about?

Rachel explained, "Each of us has our own topic of interest that we promote as our speech theme. I focus on diversity, as well as many issues important to women today, and Veronica does talks on body image. Other cast members do topics like alcohol abuse awareness or conflict resolution. Colleges love having us: they get a packed auditorium of students to listen to an important and relevant issue, and they know the only reason they filled the venue is because they have reality stars giving the speeches."

"Makes perfect sense," I said. "But how are you guys qualified to do speeches on those topics?"

"It's all based on our TV show experiences." Veronica responded. "We relate everything to personal experience, and we show clips of the shows while we're on stage and talk about what we learned from it. Plus we do a Question and Answer session after the speech, where students can talk about the topic or just ask questions about the shows and other cast members, which is typically what ends up happening."

"Sounds like a win-win for everybody." Mayo said.

Yeah, all that stuff sounded terrific in a theoretical sense, but what I was seeing in my head was cold hard dollar signs. I mean damn, if I could book both of them for an event at a college for $7,500 each—$15,000 total—my cut would be $3,000. Imagine getting a few of those per week? Shit, I'd be rich! Mayo and I had yet to determine whether we would split all the profits evenly or take the commissions for our own separate bookings, but in the meantime this was sounding like a perfect launching pad for our entertainment business.

I usually think in terms of step-by-step plans, so I went over the entire process one more time to make sure I had a handle on it: "So, we'll be calling the nightclubs and the colleges, and try to get them interested with a little sales pitch stressing the benefits of having a reality star come in, and then we'll give them a quote, try to finalize the highest possible price, and—then what? Anything else?"

"Just contact us to make sure we're available and good with the price," Veronica said. "Once we give you the green light, you send the venue an official contract with the agreed-upon terms, and that's it. Right, Rachel?"

Rachel nodded. "That's it. Just make us rich, and we'll all be happy."

"I'm sold," I said. "Mayo?"

Mayo gave a thumbs-up. "Let's do this."

As our steaks arrived, I had one last question. "You guys don't have contracts with any other agents right now?" I asked.

"Nope, we like to keep things open. We're always looking for the right agent who'll make us the most money. Hopefully that's going to be you," Veronica said.

On that optimistic note, we dug into our dinners. Those outrageously priced filets tasted amazing, probably gaining even more flavor from the exciting new business venture I was embarking on with two super-hot reality stars. In fact those steaks could have been made of cardboard and I would enjoyed every bite. I was on a high like seldom before.

During the rest of the dinner we talked about our personal lives, and got to know each other better. I had the feeling that we were all going to get along great, and that this was the start of a beautiful friendship and business partnership. But I had no idea how life-changing this first reality star meeting would be.

After dinner we all walked back to the hotel and had a few more drinks at the hotel bar. I didn't want to get too drunk my first time hanging out with Veronica and Rachel, since I wanted them to be confident that we'd make excellent and professional agents. So, after our third after-dinner round I pushed away from the bar. "It's probably time to call it a night."

Veronica and Rachel objected. "No!" These girls were used to partying, their night was just beginning.

But I wisely begged off. "We have to be at NACA early tomorrow,"

"You already found your clients, why bother?" Rachel jokingly asked.

"Because," I quickly responded, "We gotta start getting you some college gigs."

Veronica was pleased with my answer. "Good point Andy, I like the way you think. You guys work hard for us and we'll work hard for you."

"Deal!" And with that, we hugged each other goodnight, and Mayo and I went up to our room. That's right, room. With our fledgling business and limited budget, we had no choice but to share a hotel room. But after this great dinner with two top reality stars, I couldn't help but dream that one day in the near future we'd be traveling to big-money events in private jets and limos and staying in five-star suites. Maybe wishful thinking, maybe not.

Mayo and I spent the rest of the conference gathering college event leads for Veronica and Rachel, enjoying the Baltimore nightlife, and reflecting on our immense good fortune. We had decided to go to NACA on a whim, with no business plan at all, and somehow it turned out to be one of the best decisions we ever could have made.

Now I was anxious and excited to get back home, and do what I could to get Veronica and Rachel as many gigs as possible. All I could think about was that awesome twenty percent commission for every event and appearance I booked. Soon I'd be raking in the money! What Veronica and Rachel forgot to mention, and what I was about to discover for myself, was everything else that came with it. Yes, the perks were beyond anything I could've ever imagined. But so was the drama.

Flyer used at NACA to promote Veronica and Rachel's college speech events

CHAPTER 2

GIG #1: VERONICA
AND RACHEL

"HI, I'M ANDY, I REPRESENT TWO of the top reality stars from
MTV's *Real World/Road Rules Challenge* series—Veronica Portillo
and Rachel Robinson—and we're interested in coming to your
nightclub for an appearance. Can I talk to the person in charge to
see if there's an interest?"

"Yeah, hold on a minute. . . ."

After that minute—

"Hello?"

Start all over. "Hi, I'm Andy, I represent two of the top reality
stars from MTV's *Real World/Road Rules Challenge* series—
Veronica Portillo and Rachel Robinson—and we're interested in
coming to your nightclub for an appearance. They would be happy
to sign autographs and pose for pictures."

"Okay, sure—When would you like to come? We'll reserve a
table for you and give you a free round of drinks."

"Well, of course, this isn't a free appearance; the cast members get paid to come."

"Wait—we have to pay?"

"Yes, but you can promote the fact that they'll be at your club, and more people will come out that night since they'll want to meet them."

"How much?"

"We could do it for around $2,000 per reality star, it's a great deal."

"Hell no! Thanks anyway." Click.

AND THAT'S PRETTY MUCH HOW IT went at the start. Thanks but no thanks. Nightclub owners, I found, are not so eager to part with their money.

As soon as I had gotten back home from Baltimore I got right to work. I spent the whole next week googling nightclubs in dozens of cities and cold-calling them. I'd ask to speak to the manager or owner, and half the time whoever was in charge wasn't available and they took a message and I never heard from them again. When the head honcho did get on the phone, he'd listen respectfully up to the point where I mentioned the fee, and then hang up.

But I was persistent and resilient, and I plowed through call after call after call. Yes, me. You'll notice that Mayo doesn't figure substantially in this scenario. It was pretty clear from the start that the huge potential in representing reality stars excited me a lot more than Mayo. Oh, he made a few calls and did some work, but his heart was really more in the music business. He fully supported my efforts and backed me up whenever I needed him, but for the most part I had to do the heavy lifting. Fortunately I have a thick skin and can handle rejection; I was used to it from all those years chasing the ladies. Getting the brush-off from a gravelly-voiced middle-aged prick was easy by comparison.

And after a few days, I started getting somewhere. My pitch became smoother and more seductive (just like with the ladies), and I began to rope in some gigs. Within a week, we had a mini-tour of five dates put together for Veronica and Rachel. And our agency, Tobinder Talent Booking, LLC, was officially in business.

I got to write up my very first contracts (after doing a lot of research on how celebrity appearances contracts should actually look like), then sent them out to the venues to get signed. These dates averaged about $3,000 total ($1,500 each for Veronica and Rachel) per date. So I had just made my clients $15,000 for five days of appearances. That was $3,000 for me for a few days of calls. Not bad for a kid just out of college. So yeah, getting those signed contracts back from the clubs for thousands of dollars, twenty percent of which was going right into my pocket, made for an adrenaline rush that hooked me for life. I felt like the richest guy on earth. And Veronica and Rachel were so impressed with my ability to get them that much money in such a short period of time that they started giving my number to other reality stars so I could represent them too.

I was on my way.

But not too far just yet. The first date I booked for the kick-off tour was at a club called Tiki Bob's in Rochester, NY, just down the road from my home in Albany. Well, not exactly down the road—if you're familiar with the map of upstate New York, Rochester is located off the Thruway a couple of hundred miles west of Albany, and halfway between Syracuse and Buffalo—what casual observers might call the Middle of Fucking Nowhere. Who the hell wanted to go to Rochester, especially in December?

Little did I know, Rochester would end up being one of the most popular and profitable cities for reality-star events in our tour circuit. I would become very familiar with beautiful downtown Rochester—not a bad city by the way—and my wallet and I were always very happy to be there.

Still, I was a little reluctant to tell Veronica and Rachel about our first destination—they were probably expecting their new hot-shot agent to book them a sweet gig in Boston or Atlantic City—but they were pros, and game for anything. There was just one stipulation: "You're coming with us, aren't you?"

"Me?" It didn't occur to me that I would be making the trip too. After all, they'd made plenty of public appearances already, they knew how to navigate the course. I couldn't be much help to them on that score.

"That's why you need to check it out," said Veronica. "You can find out what goes on at these events, and then use what you learn to sell us to other clubs."

"Plus, you'll have fun'" said Rachel. "It's a real trip."

Well, it was only a three hour drive, and I was always down for a good time—why not? I called my partner to see if he was in.

"Mayo, you wanna go to Rochester for the kick-off of the Veronica and Rachel tour? They say it'll be a lot of fun."

"Yeah, I'm down. Will you drive?"

"I guess so." Hmm. I mean, I was going to drive anyway, but I was the one who booked these dates, and Mayo was mooching off the benefits and not even offering to drive. I was beginning to understand why good friends aren't supposed to go into business together.

Gig day arrived. Veronica and Rachel's flight was due into Rochester at 3 pm. Mayo and I left Albany around noon so we could pick them up right at the airport and then head to the hotel. As part of the contract I made sure Veronica and Rachel's flights were taken care of. I also worked out an agreement with Ray, the club owner of Tiki Bob's, to give us four comped hotel rooms, so we would each have our own private room. Living in style!

In addition, I put in a rider for Veronica and Rachel. A rider is an attachment to a celebrity's contract, listing all of the items they require at an event. Famous bands are known for having crazy over-the-top requests—the riders can run pages long with all sorts of bizarre demands for their dressing rooms. Since Veronica and Rachel weren't superstars, we couldn't push our luck too much. So I made it simple: Dinner for four, and bottle service and open bar in a VIP area with private security. Ray agreed to all our demands.

As planned, it took exactly three hours heading west on I-90 to get to the Rochester airport, and we arrived just as their plane landed. We picked our stars up and headed straight to the hotel in downtown Rochester, the Crowne Plaza. Our keycards were waiting for us when we got to the lobby.

"You're all set," said the front desk guy.

"We don't have to sign anything?" I asked. "You don't need a credit card for incidentals?"

"Nope, Ray took care of everything. We're excited to welcome you all to Rochester."

"Cool, thanks."

And yes, it was very cool. It was my first time getting this special treatment. And let me tell you, it's awesome as hell walking into a hotel, getting your keys handed to you, and going right up your room, without having to do a thing. I was beginning to think I could get used to a life of VIP treatment.

Ray had told me in advance that he wanted to bring us to dinner at 8 pm, because we had to be at the club at 11 pm. Rochester bars close at 2 am, and the contract called for a three-hour appearance. We told the girls to meet us in the lobby at 7:45; Ray planned to pick us up then for dinner.

"Will we have time after dinner to come back to the hotel and change before the club?" Veronica asked.

"I'll make sure it happens," I responded with bravado. I was feeling the Power of the Agent.

Mayo and I were happy to have our own rooms this time, and we split off to relax and get ready. I tried to take a little nap so I would be fully charged for the night's adventures, but the anticipation of my first reality star event just didn't allow for any sleep to happen. I watched a little TV, and did my preparation ritual of showering and ironing. Yes, I always iron my shirts. I don't claim to be a skilled suitcase packer, so everything is always wrinkled.

Ray called to let me know there was a lot of hype for the appearance that night, and Tiki Bob's should be slammed. He told me we were going to love the restaurant he was bringing us to, and confirmed that he'd be at the hotel as planned, right at 7:45. Perfect, I thought to myself. Everything's going like clockwork.

Mayo and I arrived in the lobby at 7:45, and to my surprise Veronica and Rachel were already there.

"Wow, right on time," I remarked.

"Hey," said Veronica, "we're professionals. When we're getting paid, there's no diva shit. We make sure we're on time for whatever the person paying us wants."

I liked the way these girls worked; it was a good business

lesson, something I absorbed and took to heart: always be professional. Well, at least try to be.

Ray was waiting in the lobby. "Andy! Great to finally meet you in person." I had spoken to Ray on the phone but this was the first time we'd met face to face. To my surprise, he wasn't a dirty middle-aged asshole club owner. He didn't have the obligatory roll of stomach hanging over his belt. No, Ray was just a few years older than me, about 6'2", and ripped.

Ray introduced me to the girl at his side. "This is my girlfriend Kelly," Ray said.

Kelly was a 5'4", gorgeous, blonde-haired, blue-eyed, perfectly tanned girl in her early twenties. It figured, a tall, muscular club-owner like Ray would get a bombshell like this.

It was my turn to make introductions. "I'd like to introduce you to Veronica and Rachel, and my business partner Mayo."

Everyone shook hands and exchanged pleasantries.

"So," said Ray, "we gotta a lot of shit to get through for tonight's event, so we won't be joining you for dinner, but everything is taken care of. I'll drop you guys off and pick you up when you're done. Order anything and everything you want. It's on us."

"Awesome, thanks man. And you can bring us back to the hotel before the club, right?" I asked.

"Of course, no prob."

Everything was no prob. I was loving it.

Fortunately Ray had a big SUV with plenty of seats. We all piled in and he drove us to this outstanding Italian restaurant.

"A lot of Italians in Rochester," Ray explained. "Some of the best Italian food you'll find in the country."

Ray walked us in and introduced us to the restaurant owner, before taking off. The owner brought us to our table and we got to work ordering drinks and apps.

"Feels like the four of us were just having dinner in Baltimore, and now we're back at it," Rachel said.

"Yeah," I said, "But this time I don't have to pay for it."

"You don't have to pay for anything tonight," Veronica smiled. "You did an amazing job getting us these gigs so fast. I definitely think this is going to be the start of a great relationship."

"And a great career for you guys in reality TV," chimed in Rachel.

"Thanks, ladies. I hope so." We drank to that.

In fact throughout the next hour we had several drinks, a nice selection of apps and some incredible Italian food, all at no charge. The whole vibe was great. Except from one little troubling aspect. . . .

About thirty seconds after the first round of appetizers arrived, Mayo rose from his chair. "Excuse me, I have to go out and make a call."

"Why now?" I asked.

"Argument with the girlfriend. Gotta talk to her."

Really? In the middle of a meal with our first clients? I was definitely starting to sense that Mayo might not be the best fit for this branch of the entertainment business.

While I was annoyed, I wasn't going to say anything; it wasn't the time and the place. But then, five minutes after he came back to the table, Mayo left again to call his girlfriend, and I saw the look on Veronica and Rachel's faces: if I was angry, they were *pissed*.

As soon as he walked away, they let me have it: "Doesn't he know how rude that is? Getting up and leaving during a meal with your clients?" Veronica asked.

"I know, he's new to this, I'll talk to him. I'm sorry about it."

"It's fine," Rachel reassured me, "but it's just rude. I'm surprised he's okay with doing that."

So they were already disenchanted with Mayo, no question about it, and I only could hope he would pull his shit together and get with the program the rest of the evening.

Mayo came back and took a seat. Everything was cool. The dinners arrived, and—Mayo got up to make *another* call. What the fuck?

"Dude!" I said out loud this time, "Are you serious? This is really rude, walking out in the middle of a meal."

"Sorry, man, gotta do it," he said, not seeming to care. And off he went. I gave the girls an apologetic shrug, and we turned to our meals. But I made a mental note that after this whole gig was over with, Mayo and I would need to have a real conversation on the proper etiquette when we're with our clients, and whether he's serious about being a part of this business.

However, Veronica and Rachel were not going to let Mayo's issues stop the good vibe of the night, and neither was I. Not when the food was this delicious. I asked the owner what the meal would've normally cost us, and he told me around $350. Damn! We drank and ate a shitload. But hey, it was my first gig ever and I wanted to take full advantage. And clearly so far I was.

Ray picked us up from dinner and brought us back to the Plaza so the girls could change for the club appearance. It was 10 pm now, and we needed to head over to Tiki Bob's by 10:45.

"Can you be ready in forty-five minutes?" I asked Veronica and Rachel.

"When money is involved, definitely." Like I said, these girls really had their business heads on straight.

Mayo and I went over to the hotel bar to have a few drinks while we waited. I decided that now was not the time to bring up the whole dinner fiasco, so we just bullshitted a while and talked about tonight's event.

"You think it'll be packed?" I asked.

"Ray says it should be."

"Hopefully it is, so he wants to do more events with us. And hopefully there'll be some hotties there too."

"They are all for you, dude, the GF is already mad at me."

"Yeah, I noticed."

We finished our drinks just as Veronica and Rachel showed up at the bar, wearing knockout dresses and looking gorgeous as hell. We stood up to leave—

"A round of shots before we head over?" Veronica suggested.

—and we sat down again. Shots were poured, we all cheered to a great night ahead, and then we walked out to meet Ray just as he was pulling up.

Tiki Bob's was only five minutes from the hotel. "Wait until you see the line, guys," said Ray. "It's nuts. We're already at capacity and there's almost an hour wait to get in."

"Hell yeah!" I said. But secretly I was wondering: is he kidding? He's gotta be kidding.

We pulled up in front of Tiki Bob's. He wasn't kidding. The line was several blocks long, and it was generously filled with girls in tiny dresses, freezing their asses off in the frigid December night.

"Wow. Sucks they have to wait outside in this cold," I commented.

"Hey, their fault for dressing like that," said Ray, talking like a typical club owner.

But he had a point. Still, I hoped the line would move quickly, since I did feel bad they were stuck out there. See, I do have a nice side. Sometimes.

We drove around to the back of the club where a huge 300-pound guy in black pants and a black shirt with "SECURITY" in white letters on the back waited for us by an open door.

"Tanto will escort you guys to the VIP area through the back entrance. He'll be with you all night to make sure there are no issues," Ray told us.

"Hi, Tanto," I said cheerfully.

"Hello," said Tanto, without a smile. He was one of those men of few words who can scare the shit out of you without even trying. I was glad he was on our side.

"Okay, I gotta park the car," said Ray. "I'll catch up with you in a few minutes. Have fun!"

"Sounds good, thanks Ray."

Ray took off, and we turned to our man Tanto. "This way," he said flatly, and headed inside. Tanto wasn't knocking us out with his personality, but we could tell we were in good hands with him.

The four of us followed him through a back hallway, and we entered the club behind the bar. Tanto guided us to our roped-off VIP area, where there were complimentary bottles waiting. It was surreal, the whole experience: getting whisked through the back entrance of a nightclub and escorted by our own personal bouncer to a private VIP area, with free liquor, AND getting paid for it!

A buzz went through Tiki Bob's as people started noticing Veronica and Rachel's presence. Fans began to gather around the rope that blocked the VIP area. The imposing Tanto kept pushing the gawkers back, not letting them get too close. Which was certainly appreciated, but Veronica and Rachel were getting paid to meet their fans, and I wanted to make sure that happened at some point. But at *this* point, I was happy to crack open a bottle of Grey Goose and pour out mixed drinks for all. The four of us hung out and talked and drank and checked out the crowd, while we waited for Ray to check in with us.

"Good-looking crowd," Veronica observed. "Andy, you're single, right?"

"Yes I am."

"We got you."

I wasn't sure what that meant, but I liked the sound of it.

Just then, Ray showed up at the VIP area with Kelly, and laid out his battle plan to make sure we were cool with it:

"OK, so how about we announce that you're both here, and we get you guys standing on the bar, and you can pour shots into the customers' mouths for a few minutes? After that we'll do a meet-and-greet line for anybody who wants to take pictures with you. Then we'll bring you back here to the VIP and you can just chill and drink the rest of the night. Sound like a plan?"

"Works for us." Rachel said.

Tanto pushed through the crowd as if he were parting the Red Sea, and we all followed him to an area behind the bar. Ray introduced us to the very hot bartenders, and then handed Veronica and Rachel each a wireless microphone and a bottle of some unidentifiable colored watered-down liquor. Tanto helped the two ladies up on the bar, and the DJ stopped the music and made the big announcement:

"Ladies and Gentleman! MTV's Veronica and Rachel are in the house! Let's show them some Rochester love!"

The packed club let loose with a cheer, as the patrons pushed their way as close to the bar as they could get. Veronica and Rachel looked down at their excited fans with a calm radiance, totally poised; they were a couple of stars.

"Rochester NY!" Veronica shouted into her mic, and the crowd cheered happily for itself. "We're so happy to be here!"

"You gonna show us that Rochester people know how to PARTY?!" Rachel asked.

Another raucous cheer. This was awesome. I was feeding off the excitement.

"We want to thank Ray for bringing us here to Tiki Bob's, and also our agent Andy who's with us tonight." Veronica pointed me out. "Andy, wave to the crowd!"

I waved from behind the bar and the crowd cheered again. Shit, this was really amazing.

"Okay guys, we're partying with you all night long, so let's start the festivities by doing some shots!" Rachel shouted. She held her bottle aloft. "Come on over!"

The DJ turned the music back up as the girls started pouring shots into every open mouth until the bottles were empty. It didn't take long. Tanto helped them back down from the bar as the DJ told everyone to line up if they wanted a picture with Veronica and Rachel.

We were escorted to where the line was forming. As expected, I ended up being the makeshift camera guy; everyone would hand me their cameras when they got to the front of the line so I could take a picture of them with Veronica and Rachel. I didn't mind, it was part of my job. And it paid a very sweet dividend. Every time a hot girl came up for a picture, Veronica would say,

"Hey, did you meet our agent Andy? He's the best!"

"He's the shit!" added Rachel.

It was like a magic incantation. Every time I got that build-up, the previously-indifferent hot chick was suddenly all into me, asking for my number and saying we should meet up and party after the club closed. Yeah, I was down!

See, this type of stuff never happened to me before. I was 5'8" and average-looking, and accordingly I always kept my expectations manageable. But these girls giving me all this attention and wanting to hang with me, they were all tens. It was the New Math, and I was loving every second of it.

As promised in their contracts, Veronica and Rachel chatted with everyone who waited in line to meet them. It took about an hour. We then went back over to the VIP area and drank some more.

I made sure to thank Veronica. "You're officially the best wing-girl a guy could ask for."

"Hey, you take care of us, we take care of you."

We invited a few of the local girls into the VIP area and did some more shots. Mayo was still occupied with his phone calls, but Veronica, Rachel and I were having a blast. I was drinking for free with two famous reality stars, and a handful of hot girls who wanted to party with me, all while getting paid. How was this real life?

Just as I was thinking I'd better take a break from the shots so I don't get too drunk at my first gig, Ray came over and mentioned that he still had to pay me.

"Of course," I said, "Thanks for reminding me." To be honest, in all the excitement I *had* forgotten. I made a mental note for future gigs: always ask for the balance of the cash right away. Ray seemed like a trustworthy guy, but you never know with some club owners. Imagine if we did the whole appearance and then they refused to pay us at the end of the night? I'd be stuck with a huge hassle, dealing with lawyers and lawsuits and all that.

Fortunately, Ray had it all waiting for me when we got to his office. "So, we already sent you the fifty percent deposit, so we owe you $1,500 cash, right?" Ray asked.

"That is correct," I responded, trying not to slur my words since I was starting to feel the effect of the shots.

Ray counted out fifteen one hundred dollar bills and handed them to me.

"Here you go. Let's definitely do this again. You guys are great to work with," he said.

"You too, Ray." I said, happily putting the money in my pocket. "Definitely looking forward to coming back!"

Somehow it was now 1:40 am. The three hours at the club felt like ten minutes. I walked back over to the crew in the VIP area and told Veronica and Rachel we'd be leaving in a few. We all had one more drink, and a couple of my new lady friends from Rochester—Brittney and Ashley—asked if they could meet me at our hotel after. Sounded like a great idea to me.

At 2 am on the dot, Tiki Bob's started closing up, and Ray met us in VIP to drive us back to the Crowne Plaza. I told Brittney and Ashley to call me when they got to the hotel, and then our entourage followed Tanto out through the back hall to the back exit where Ray's SUV was waiting, the engine running and the heat blasting. We all shook Tanto's hand, and he gave us a head nod and walked away. Just another night's work for the big man.

On the ride back to the Plaza we all complimented Ray and his crew at Tiki Bob's, and he gave it back to us by saying everything went perfect and thanked us again for coming. As we got out of the car, he assured us we'd be working with him again real soon. Ray drove off, and we hustled out of the cold night into the hotel.

"So," Veronica asked as we walked into the lobby, "What did you think of your first reality-star gig?"

I tried to find the words. "Let's see—we partied for free in the VIP section with some amazing people, and we got paid for it. I'm officially addicted."

"Just keep getting us the money and you'll be doing a lot more of that," Rachel added.

Sounded like an excellent plan to me.

At that moment my phone rang.

"Hey Andy! It's Brittney and Ashley. You still down to party? We're pulling up to the hotel now."

"Definitely. I'm waiting for you in the lobby." I hung up, and looked at Veronica and Rachel. "Brittney and Ashley," I explained.

They raised their eyebrows with amusement. "They didn't waste much time," said Veronica.

"I guess they liked what they saw," teased Rachel.

"Thanks again for hooking me up," I said.

"Happy to do so. You deserve it, Mr. Agent Man."

Rachel yawned. "But we're gonna head to bed. Can you handle the ladies without us?"

"I think so," I said.

"Yeah, I'm going up too," Mayo said. "My girl is still pissed off at me."

"Wow, you'd better call her," I said with mock concern. Mayo didn't pick up on the dig, but Veronica and Rachel did, and both gave me knowing smiles.

We all said goodnight, and they headed off to the elevator. A minute later two of the hottest girls I've ever had the pleasure of meeting walked into the lobby.

"Andy! Thanks for tonight, we had so much fun," Brittany said.

"Any time, ladies." I noticed a bottle of vodka in Ashley's hand. "I see you came prepared."

"We did!" Ashley said. "I hope you're down for some drinking games."

"What kind of drinking games?" I asked.

"The X-rated kind," she said.

I started to smile. "Oh I think I could be down for that." (By the way, this dialogue is 100 percent accurate. I swear. Really).

The three of us headed for the elevator, passing the guy on the overnight shift at the front desk. He shot me a look that clearly said: "I absolutely hate you, and I absolutely wish I was you." I know, because I've been that guy. And I always wondered what it felt like to be the lucky bastard everybody else hated. Now I knew. It felt great.

As we got off the elevator and headed down the hall to my room, I put my arms around Brittney and Ashley and couldn't stop smiling. I was now officially a reality star agent, I'd just made myself hundreds of dollars for one event, and I was having the best night of my life so far. And it was only just beginning.

CHAPTER 3

THE WORLD OF "REAL" AND THE Z-LIST

As I began to focus on my newfound career, I figured I should take some time to fully understand this "reality" world I'd just jumped into. Sure, like everybody else of my generation I had at least a passing acquaintance with reality shows, and I knew who the big stars of the genre were. I recognized Veronica and Rachel the minute they approached me in Baltimore, and I knew that they'd first made a splash in the reality show *Road Rules* and subsequently went on to star in a number of *Real World/Road Rules Challenges*. So I wasn't completely unaware of the major players, but at the same time I wasn't an ultra-fan who devoured every season and knew every little detail about each series and every cast member. I had better things to do.

Except now I didn't. Now it was my paycheck and my life-blood. And if I planned to represent these stars and get them the best deals, I needed to know where they stood in the celebrity galaxy, and what they were likely to generate in fan ardor and, more important, monetary potential. I wanted to stake my claim as the guy who knew the reality-show world inside out, the Agent of Choice for stars eager to spin their fame into some lucrative paydays on the side.

So began the research phase of my education. I turned on the TV and opened up the computer, and immersed myself in the world of reality television. Reality shows had exploded over the last few years, and like most viewers I had assumed that the show that started it all was *Survivor*, the CBS show that debuted in 2000 and introduced us to the Darwinian world of tribes, immunity idols, secret alliances and subsequent backstabbing, and the household phrase "being voted off the island." The show was a massive success, spawning all kinds of offshoots and copies, and it's still running today. It's the quintessential reality show.

But it wasn't the first. The one that really got the ball rolling, the granddaddy of them all, the first true reality show, was *The Real World*, which debuted on MTV way back in 1992. In its first season *The Real World* brought together a group of seven strangers in New York City and did non-stop taping of their lives over the course of several months. It became an instant hit, and new seasons followed every year, filmed in different cities all over the country and the world.

By now *The Real World* has become iconic, claiming a permanent spot in pop culture history, with its colorful characters and outrageous situations. But when the show first came out it was mainly known for pushing the envelope and bringing taboo subjects into the mainstream. Viewers witnessed cast members struggling with very real issues including abortion, sexuality, AIDS, prejudice, death, and substance abuse. It was only as the years went on—by the time I landed right in the middle of this world—that the show had become more-well known for highlighting relationships and sex, immoral behavior, immaturity and irresponsibility of the youth of today. The rule-breaking, risk-taking excitement of those early seasons was gone.

Honestly, I could not care less. Some of these more recent cast members may have been on the shallow side, but they could be my ticket to the big time, and I studied them as carefully as if they were specimens under a microscope.

Road Rules premiered three years after *Real World*, in 1995, and lasted for fourteen seasons before it went to the graveyard in 2007. But the spin-off from both *Real World* and *Road Rules*— *The Challenge*—premiered in 1998 and is still going strong, with more than thirty seasons under its belt! *The Challenge* features a mix of cast members from past seasons of *Real World, Are You The One,* and *Road Rules* when that series was still on air. It was the groundwork done by these legendary reality shows that laid the foundation for dozens of hugely popular shows to come, like *Big Brother, The Bachelor, and Jersey Shore.*

Of course, the central conundrum of a reality show is that it's all real, and yet none of it's real. Only the show-runners can tell you how much of any particular show is scripted, but believe me, every one of them is guided into certain directions and plot points for the purposes of developing a juicy storyline and fulfilling audience expectations. Hey, they're spending a lot of money on these shows, they have to have some control over them.

Still, the characters aren't played by professional actors (that's pretty obvious), they're real people; and how they're going to react to the situations thrown at them is the great unknowable. Some rise to the occasion and cover themselves with glory; others crash and burn in a public spectacle of degradation to rival the Roman Circuses.

But whether they were superstars or laughingstocks, heroes or clowns—as long as they were bankable, I wanted them in my stable. And I started feeling much more qualified in my position now that I had a little background on the shows that featured my clients. When friends and family would ask what I was doing with my life, there would be a genuine pride in my voice when I responded that I represented some of the stars of reality TV. It was definitely an exciting time, and I had the impression that there was no limit to where this could bring me. Reality TV was a permanent and influential part of popular culture, and it wasn't going anywhere.

Now I would be the first to admit that these were not huge mega-celebrities I was representing. Sure, I wanted my friends to be amazed by my rising fortunes and my success in the entertainment world, but I wasn't kidding myself. I knew that so-and-so wasn't an A-list actor or a top-rung musician. I would treat them as such, make sure they felt special, and make them as much money as possible. But as I learned more about these shows and their "stars", both past and present, I became more cognizant of their place in the show-business hierarchy. If they weren't A-listers, what were they? B-listers? Hell, there were real actors and actresses who didn't make the A-list cut but were far more famous and talented than these reality stars. Truth be told, they weren't even C-listers. No, these folks belonged in a separate category of their own:

THE Z-LIST

What's a Z-lister? To me, it's someone who's famous for being famous. He or she hasn't really accomplished anything of great value in the entertainment world, and doesn't have much (if any) artistic talent. Despite that sobering fact, this very ordinary person is idolized and obsessed over as if some divine creature had alighted to Earth. Rabid fans can't get enough of her, whether by watching her every week on TV, or by waiting in line for hours at an event for a chance to meet her. Through some weird alchemy, reality television combines enormous fame and minimal talent to produce the singular figure that I call the Z-list celebrity.

Not that I would call them that to their faces. They all have healthy, publicity-fed egos, and it would be cruel to them, as well as counter-productive to my own career, to cast any aspersions on their accomplishments. But privately, I did begin to ponder how strange it was that I was now making a living by representing celebrities who had done nothing in particular worth celebrating. At this point I wasn't going to look a gift horse in the mouth, but still, I couldn't help wondering, what's to come? Would all of the Z-listers be as nice as Veronica and Rachel? Or would their egos inflate under all that attention, and lead them to expect adoration, ass-kissing, and VIP treatment everywhere they went?

I would find out soon enough.

CHAPTER 4
THE ROSTER EXPANDS

EARLY SUCCESS LED TO MORE OPPORTUNITY. I was getting Veronica and Rachel gig after gig, and they started telling their reality-star friends that there was a new agent in town, and he was a hustler.

Which I was. Even though I was only just getting out of the blocks, I was already looking for interesting angles to exploit. The next major NACA conference was coming up in Minneapolis, and I had a great idea: I would install a top MTV reality star in my booth, to attract as many people as possible. Hopefully once these college student leaders and their advisors checked out my set-up, they would want to book some reality stars. A foolproof scheme—but who would I bring? It's not like I had a shitload of clients. Veronica and Rachel had already done the NACA scene, they didn't need to do that dog-and-pony show anymore (thanks to me). But maybe I could ask them to hook me up with one of their friends in the biz...?

It was just while I was revolving this plan in my mind that the phone rang, the ID showing a Wisconsin area code. Who did I know in Wisconsin?

"Andy! What's up, my man?" said an energetic male voice.

"That depends," I said warily. "Who's this?"

"This is Landon Lueck, I'm from MTV's *Real World Philadelphia...*?"

Landon Lueck! I didn't need any research to know who he was. At this time, 2005, *Real World Philadelphia* was one of the hottest and highest-rated reality shows on TV. Landon was the breakaway star of the show, the guy the ladies went wild for. I sensed immediate potential.

"Hey, Landon!" I said, as if we were old friends. "How you doin'? What's up?"

"Well, I got your number from Veronica Portillo. She said you're her agent and that you do a kick-ass job."

Thanks again, V. "Well, I do what I can."

"So, you wanna work with me?"

This could not have been more serendipitous. I didn't waste any time putting my plan into action:

"Actually it's funny you should call just now, Landon. I'm going to the National Association of Campus Activities conference in a few weeks, and I was looking for a major reality star to join our booth. And that's certainly you. I could probably get you some nice gigs out of it. Basically we're talking about a meet-and-greet that's a few hours long for a couple of days. You take pictures with potential decision makers, and I solidify the deals, and we both make money. Interested?"

"Fuck yeah I am, let's do it."

Well, that was easy enough. I agreed to pay for Landon's transportation and hotel room; as a businessman I know you have to spend money to make money. And I wanted to keep him happy and continue spreading the word to fellow reality stars: hey, you need an agent?—Andy's the man.

So that was the good news: Landon was set. The bad news? Well, just as I expected, my buddy Mayo had no desire to go to Minneapolis in the winter. In fact, he'd decided it was time to say goodbye to the whole business. He just didn't have the Z-list passion that I did. Mayo was a music guy: he wanted to be in charge of huge concerts in major arenas. We parted ways amicably, and he still joined in every so often at future NACA conferences to help out a little, since we always had a good time doing it. To this day we've stayed great friends and, no surprise, he has since fulfilled his own dream of working for the biggest concerts in the country as a bigwig for a major promoter. He's my source for free tickets often. And he even ended up marrying that girlfriend that wouldn't stop calling him during dinner with Veronica and Rachel.

Anyway, Mayo or not, I still had high hopes for my NACA experience with Landon. I flew into Minneapolis on a cold-ass February day with a smile on my face, ready to conquer. My friends and family back home were saying I was nuts to go to Minneapolis in February (as if Albany is much better). But first of all, dollar signs were drawing me there. Secondly, if you're unfamiliar with Minneapolis, it's actually set up that you barely have to walk outside when it's cold. Almost every building in the city is connected by heated enclosed walkways. You can literally go from one end of the city to the other without stepping foot outside. So it really wasn't bad at all.

My flight arrived about four hours before Landon was scheduled to be there. Fortunately all of my boxes of promo materials and the banner for my booth made it to baggage claim. I got a cart, found a cab, and headed to the hotel and conference center in downtown. It was a hassle setting up the booth myself without Mayo, but I made it work. I met some other really interesting college entertainment hopefuls while I was setting up in the exhibit hall. It looked like this was going to be just like NACA in Baltimore was, only bigger.

A few hours later, after I was all set up and sitting at the hotel bar having a drink, I got a call from Landon. "Andy! I just got in. I should be at the hotel in half-an-hour." Great, no issues getting in. The typical worry of a missed or cancelled flight had fortunately been allayed.

"Awesome—I'll meet you in the lobby, and I'll have your room key ready." My plan for this first meeting was to really kiss his ass and make things as smooth as possible for him. This particular Z-lister was more well-known than many A-listers at that moment, and I wanted him to know that he was a valued client. Especially since I hadn't booked him for any gigs yet.

A half hour later Landon walked into the hotel lobby. I recognized him right away.

"Landon! What's up, man? I'm Andy."

"Andy!" He shook my hand. "I'm excited to be here—let's make some loot!"

"Hell yeah, that's the plan!"

I walked him up to his room, and we met in the lobby an hour later for a pre-conference drink. After talking with him for just a few minutes I knew we'd get along great. We had similar interests: making money, drinking, and girls. Granted, most guys in their mid-20s had the same interests, but still, he was extremely friendly and down-to-earth; he wasn't letting his overnight fame get to him.

We finished our beers and walked over to the exhibit hall. The agents and artists are allowed in the exhibit hall 30 minutes before it opens up to the conference attendees. Hundreds of colleges would be represented from around the country, so I knew it would be a madhouse once the doors opened. I explained the deal to Landon:

Landon and Andy pregaming in a hotel before a nightclub appearance

"These are students from their College Activities or Events Boards, they have big budgets and they make the decisions on what events to bring to campus. They'll probably be with their advisors—the advisors sign off on the contracts once the students make the decisions. These kids will already be excited to meet you, and then we seal the deal with the advisors by explaining how you can speak on a relevant campus issue, and your celebrity will draw a lot of students who wouldn't normally come."

Landon wanted to base his talks on Alcohol Awareness. He'd had some drinking issues on the show, and his game plan was to show clips of his troubled days and then talk to the students about how he's grown from that and the lessons it's taught him. Would be a win-win for everyone: the students get to meet a super-famous reality star, and the campus gets a packed house to come hear lessons on alcohol abuse awareness. And we get paid.

"Sounds good to me," Landon responded.

"Okay, so just be nice to everyone, take pictures with anyone who asks, tell them that you want to come to their campus and then send them over to me to finalize details."

"Done."

The doors opened, and I watched as the conference-goers flooded in. And there must have been a tilt in the floor, because for some reason a lot of those bright-eyed college kids were flooding right towards my booth! I couldn't believe it! Holy shit, what a difference from Baltimore! Last time at NACA Mayo and I barely talked to anyone other than Veronica and Rachel. Now I had easily the longest line of people in the entire conference waiting at my booth waiting to meet Landon. No exaggeration: it was the entire length of the conference hall. People stretched down the entire row, blocking other booths along the way.

Which meant I was constantly getting yelled at by conference staff and other companies; we were apparently causing chaos and obstructing visitors from going to the other booths. I felt really bad about this. Oh well.

It was amazing. We couldn't keep up: picture after picture, contact after contact, so many campuses interested in booking Landon. The Alcohol Awareness-plus-reality star combo was a slam-dunk home run. The session lasted about two hours, but it felt like ten minutes. When it was over I had close to hundred colleges expressing interest in booking Landon. We left the exhibit hall in an amazing mood, went right back to the hotel bar, got a cocktail, mingled with some groupies, and then got ready to do it all over again the next day.

We had a great time in Minneapolis fielding potential gigs and getting to know each other. But once the conference was over, it was time for me to get to work and solidify some of these dates. Yeah, I had over 100 leads, but the real skill comes in finalizing the deals and making the most money possible. I told Landon I'd give him an update in a week, if there was any news. Little did I know—within two days of making calls I had 20 colleges locked in! I couldn't believe how easy it was. And they were paying WAY more than the nightclubs of the Veronica and Rachel gigs. Landon was averaging $5,000 per event. And my commission was 20%. So $1,000 per event, times 20 gigs…I just made around $20,000 in two days. Holy shit!

I called Landon each time a new date came in, to confirm he could do it. He was loving every call, and ultimately decided to put together his own website—another brilliant move. Landon proved to be a genius at self-branding, posting shirtless pictures all over his website, along with a link to the tour page with all of the dates we had just booked …and another link to buy a Landon-themed calendar, featuring a picture of Landon for every month. The site is long gone now (in case you were looking for those shirtless pics) but in its day, landonlueck.net was as hot a celebrity website as you could get.

We booked dates all over the country. I wasn't planning to attend every one, but I definitely wanted to check out a few of the early gigs, to make sure things were going well, and also to show Landon that I supported him. In order to minimize my expenses, I picked out bookings that I could drive to.

The first one within a 5-hour driving distance was in the middle of nowhere Pennsylvania. I met Landon at the hotel, and we commenced what was to become our regular routine—an opening drink at the hotel bar. I broke out the contract, just to make sure he had everything in place.

"Andy, I know the drill. You're not going to be at every gig. I can handle it."

"I know, but this is my first one with you, so humor me."

He smiled with a shrug, and sipped his drink as I proceeded.

"So—the college is picking us up here at 6 pm and bringing us to dinner. "

"Let me guess—Applebee's?" Landon asked.

"Ha! How'd you know?"

He rolled his eyes. "More than half the colleges I visit want to take me to Applebee's for dinner. I have no idea why they all love it so much. I'm sick of that place."

"I'm not a fan either but, you know—for $5,000, we eat where they want. "

"Yeah yeah, I know."

"I think there'll be five members from the student campus activities board joining us. They'll ask you a million questions at dinner, I'm sure, so be nice."

"I'm always nice."

"After dinner we go straight to the campus. We should have about thirty minutes to chill in the dressing room. At 8 pm you do your speech about alcohol awareness..." I paused to watch him finish his drink and order a round of shots. "... and then we do a Q & A, followed by a meet-and-greet. After that we're free to do whatever we want."

"Works for me!" Landon held up his glass, and I joined him in throwing back a shot. We went over to the hotel lobby to wait for our ride to the campus, so that Landon could inform the students about the dangers of alcohol. Clearly his research was ongoing.

Five minutes later a heavyset but very nice girl named Sophie hobbled into the hotel. She introduced herself as the student president of the campus activities board. I, in turn, introduced her to Landon.

"So nice to meet you, Sophie,' said Landon, putting out his hand and smiling with full-dimple charm, "and thank you so much for having me tonight." As she took his hand, I could see every large bone in her body melting. "I'm super excited to be here," he went on. "We're gonna have an amazing time!"

Sophie couldn't talk for a few seconds, but she finally found her voice. "Oh, Landon, we're so happy to have you, and thank you so much for coming! I've watched every episode of your season, I'm probably your biggest fan!"

"Well, I'm *your* biggest fan," the ultra-kind Landon quickly responded.

When Sophie stopped blushing, we followed her outside to see a white mini-van idling, with the college's name on the side.

"Riding in style," I whispered to Landon.

Landon got in the front seat—always his preference—and I squeezed into the back with four other students from the activities board. I don't know if any of these kids had showered in several days, but the stench inside the car was almost unbearable.

Sophie, as she got in the driver's seat and pulled away, introduced her group. There was Charlie, Peg, and Kevin—all Landon Lueck mega-fans, each of whom took up more space in the van than Sophie.

And then there was Kaitlyn. One of these things was not like the others. Kaitlyn was gorgeous!

Landon and I were both talkative and pleasant to everyone, but damn, that Kaitlyn was sexy. As we got out of our foul smelling mini-van in the Applebee's parking lot and walked to the main entrance, I strolled up next to Kaitlyn.

"Is there anything to do in this town on a random Tuesday night?"

"Not really. There's one bar that's not bad." Kaitlyn said.

"One bar is all I need. You down to drink with us after?" I asked.

"Definitely!"

Nice, she was in, and hopefully she would bring some friends. We all sat down at Applebee's and ordered waters and Cokes. No drinks in front of the students—they might perceive a disconnect with Landon's anti-alcohol presentation.

As a rule many activities board members aren't your typical college partiers, and most of our van-mates met that criterion. When it was time to order the meals, Landon got his Applebee's staple, a salad of some sort—had to keep his legendary rock-hard physique in check. Mine was not so legendary, so I ordered Riblets.

We chatted a little about the college. Sophie said she expected the auditorium, which fits 700 people, to be completely filled tonight. Supposedly there had been a Landon buzz on campus for the past month. Nice!

Dinner was mediocre at best—no surprise. But the price was right (we weren't paying), and I got to know Kaitlyn a little more, which was awesome. She was a senior majoring in communications, and she wanted to do something in my field after she graduated.

"Oh, I'll definitely try to help you out. Take my number and keep in touch," I told her, smoothly and confidently.

After dinner we hopped back in the smelly mini-van and headed to the event. Campus security took over when we got inside and brought us to Landon's dressing room. It was stocked with water, soda, juice, a veggie tray, a deli tray, chips and more. I didn't even ask for this stuff. And we didn't need it because we just had dinner. "Look at all this food!" I told the security guy. "Who's going to eat it?"

"Don't worry, somebody will," said the security guy with certainty. "We got plenty of students with big appetites who'll be happy to clean it up. It won't go to waste."

I knew what he meant. I was a college student myself not long ago.

Anyway, the drinks were nice, and we might be hungry after the speech so it didn't hurt to have it there. We thanked the security guy, who said he'd wait outside the door to make sure no wild fans barged in. I wasn't too worried, but hey, better to be safe.

I told Landon I was going to go check out the crowd, and walked down the backstage hall and out into the auditorium. Holy shit! Sophie wasn't kidding. The entire venue was full, and there were even students standing in the back. I knew *The Real World* was a huge hit and Landon was at the top of his game, but I wasn't expecting this kind of turnout. It totally fueled my energy and excitement as I thought about all the gigs and money, and girls, to come.

At 5 minutes to show-time Sophie appeared at the dressing room door. I handed her a DVD. "This needs to be queued up so Landon can play the clips during the speech." The DVD contained clips from *The Real World* where Landon was clearly drunk and doing ridiculous and embarrassing things. His goal: to show the students how stupid he was, and how he learned from his mistakes and what he's done about it.

Sophie in turn handed me a remote so that Landon could start and stop the DVD from the stage. Everything seemed good to go, except one thing: Money. The contract always calls for payment *before* the "Talent" takes the stage.

"Do you have the check, Sophie?" I asked.

"Oh yeah! I almost forgot, sorry!" She reached into her pocket and took out a folded envelope. "Here you go."

There it was, an official check from the college for $5,000, made out to my company, Tobinder Talent Booking, LLC. A beautiful sight.

"Perfect, thanks!" I said, tucking it away. "So, are you going to introduce Landon?" Usually the students in charge liked to go on stage and introduce the reality stars before they came out, and also give a little plug to their organization, highlighting the cool things they do and encouraging more students to join.

"Not me, I'm too nervous to be on stage," she said.

"Why? You'd be great up there!" I told her. "We'll give you the exact words to say, you can just read it."

"No, thanks—can you do it?"

"What about another student leader?" I asked. I wouldn't mind seeing Kaitlyn up there.

"No, they're all sitting down already. I'd really like it if you did it, Andy."

"Well..." Of course secretly I was happy to do it. I loved the idea of being out on stage. I just wished those 700 people were there to see *me*. But standing in the spotlight introducing my boy Landon would do for now. "If you really want me to, I guess I can. You know, happy to help out."

"Great, thank you!" Sophie said, relieved. She left to take her seat.

Landon strolled out of the dressing room, amused. "So Andy, ready for your moment of stardom?"

"I was born ready."

"Do you need me to tell you what to say?"

"Nope, I'll wing it. Let's hope for the best."

We walked down the hall to the stage entrance. A staffer radioed to lower the house lights. The lights dimmed and the screaming began, the decibel range suddenly shooting off the charts.

I couldn't believe the response. "Damn, Landon! You're at Backstreet Boys status."

"Yeah, I'm a Backstreet Boy who can't sing or dance," he said.

"A star with no talent?" I asked jokingly. He told me to shut up and get on stage to introduce him.

So I walked out on stage—simple enough, right? Not exactly. It was my first time in a spotlight, and it was literally blinding. I couldn't see anything, just the light and a sea of blackness just beyond it. I knew there were hundreds of people out there, I could hear them, but I couldn't make them out. I could barely keep my eyes open, the glare was so bright. Still, I had a job to do, so I rolled with it.

"What's up, Pennsylvania?!" I shouted into the mic.

The crowd of college students screamed.

"My name's Andy, and I'm Landon's agent, and we're so happy to be here tonight!"

The crowd screamed louder.

"Who's excited to see Landon?" I shouted, channeling my inner rock star.

The crowd screamed again.

"Oh, come on. Landon is backstage right now, but he won't come out until you're loud enough. I said, who's excited to see Landon?!"

This time, the crowd roared like a freight train. It was time.

"That's what I wanna hear! Okay, so it is my honor to introduce to you tonight, the STAR of MTV's *Real World Philadelphia,* and the best looking guy I know, please welcome, reality TV legend, LANDON LUECK!!!"

The crowd screamed again with excitement and Landon walked out on stage. We crossed paths as I made my way off stage—I shook his hand and handed him the mic.

"You're a natural," he whispered into my ear.

I smiled and walked over to the side of the stage, out of sight of the crowd, to watch.

Actually Landon was the real natural. It was so cool watching him in action on stage. He was totally professional, and a great speaker. Landon talked about his journey to the show, his mistakes, what he's learned, and how he planned to move forward with his life. Seeing himself on TV, acting in certain ways, was so embarrassing to him, he told the crowd, that he never wanted to be like that again. No more drunken nights. Responsible drinking only.

The students all seemed mesmerized by him, and nodded their heads in agreement with everything he was saying. I met the staff advisor from the college briefly during the speech, and he was very pleased. My selling point had rung true: 700 students, of their own free will, coming to learn about the dangers of drinking. Had Professor Joe Schmoe given the speech, the head count would have been closer to 7.

After the hour-long speech, Landon gave the students a chance to ask questions. For about 30 minutes, the topics ranged from the sobering statistics of alcohol abuse, to the far more pressing question of how many reality star cast members he'd fucked. He took them all in stride, answering most of them, deflecting a few. As any politician would.

After the Q and A, it was time for the meet and greet. I joined Landon on stage to help with pictures, and everyone who wanted to meet him lined up in the auditorium, and Sophie sent them on stage one by one to get a picture and autograph. They of course handed me the camera when they came up, I took the picture, they talked to Landon for a few seconds telling him how amazing his speech was and how huge of fans they were, and then they walked off stage. Repeat, repeat, repeat for about an hour. It was exhausting but we were happy to do it. Being so nice and professional and popular was the reason Landon kept getting booked on the college circuit.

At the end of the line were the Mini-van Five—Sophie, Charlie, Peg, Kevin, and my dream girl Kaitlyn. Sophie asked if I could take a group shot of them with Landon.

"Of course," I said. They gathered around him, beaming with delight. "Okay everyone say: Landon is sexy."

"Landon is sexy!" they said in unison, smiling.

As Sophie went to get the van, Kaitlyn pulled me aside. "Do you guys still wanna meet up at the bar?"

Music to my ears. "Definitely!" We arranged to meet there in about an hour. She was going to bring some friends. Nice.

Sophie dropped Landon and me off at the hotel and we thanked her again said our goodbyes. Now that the business part was over, it was time for some fun.

We both went up to our rooms to spray on a little cologne and do a shot from my bottle of Jägermeister. The drink of choice for hotel pre-gaming would change throughout the years, but in those days it was most definitely Jäger.

The hotel shuttle was taking us to the bar in about twenty minutes, so we just bullshitted for a few, talking about how great the gig was, and what the rest of the night might bring. Of course I brought up my dream girl: "I'm sure Kaitlyn wants you tonight, but give me a chance." I said.

Landon knew he would have his hands full, so he could afford to be generous. "She's all yours, man."

We headed back down to the lobby where the shuttle was waiting. As we drove off, there was one question I had to ask: "Landon, isn't it weird that you just did an alcohol abuse awareness speech and now we're going out drinking?"

"Not really. It's not like I'm gonna get hammered. At least I don't think I am."

The shuttle driver, an older guy, looked over his shoulder at us, and did a little double-take.

"Landon Lueck, right? What are you doing in our little ass town?"

That caught us by surprise. "You're a fan of *Real World*?" I asked.

"My daughter watches it every week, so I try to keep up with it since it gives us something to talk about. Hey, you're one cool dude, Landon."

"Thanks, man," Landon said. "So are you."

When we got to the bar, Landon posed for a picture with the driver, and signed something for him to give to his daughter. There was another surprise waiting for us at the bar entrance: There was a long, long line to get in. Apparently this *was* the only bar in town.

I walked over to the huge, mean-looking bouncer in front. He had his arms folded, with a nasty scowl on his face. It didn't look promising, but I turned on the charm.

"Hey man, my name's Andy."

"My name's Pinch," he answered, without a hint of a smile. "And the line is back there."

"Well—look, Pinch, I have Landon from MTV's *Real World* with me. Any chance we can go right in?"

The surly bouncer turned into a gushing fan in an instant. "Oh shit! Landon! Hey, what's up, Landon? Yeah of course you guys can head right in. Give me a minute, I'll set up a private VIP area for you too!"

Not only did we get the VIP section, but Micky the owner gave us a free bar tab, and another bouncer for security protection for the night. Damn, these perks were amazing.

Plenty of girls were hovering around our blocked-off VIP area, and of course we invited the hot ones in to have some drinks with us. In the meantime, I kept an eye out for Kaitlyn, who finally showed up with an entourage of five beautiful girls. Our roped-off area was pretty small, so I politely told the other girls that we needed to make room for some new people, but that Landon would hang out again later.

"Okay, but can we party with you guys at the hotel later?" one of them asked me.

"Yeah, of course." I gave her my number and the hotel and said to meet us there around 2 am (when the bars close in Pennsylvania).

Now Kaitlyn and her crew entered our inner sanctum, and she gave me a hug and introduced us to her friends. Once the formalities were out of the way, we got down to serious drinking.

And damn, this girl could drink. She downed shot after shot, easily out-drinking Landon and I. I even told her, "Hey, slow down, Kaitlyn, we have the whole night ahead of us."

Unfortunately she didn't. Before I knew it, she was passed out, head down on the table, her friends saying they needed to get her home. We had Pinch escort them to a cab to make sure she got home okay.

So my Kaitlyn dream was dashed. Maybe our paths would cross another day.

No worries though, since the ladies were everywhere. And within seconds of seeing Kaitlyn's crew leave, the original group hanging out with us earlier was back at the rope. The leader was waving at me frantically. "Yo, hello—can we get back in?"

"Yeah, sure—what's your name again?"

"It's Jen!" she yelled crossly. "I told you three times already!"

"OK, sorry! We meet a lot of people. No need to get mad about it."

After we had another drink with them, Landon and I came to the same realization: these girls were just way too annoying. Yes, they were hot, but hot isn't everything—not if you can't stand listening to them talk.

Landon was giving me a look that was easy to decipher: get rid of these girls. So I nicely told them we had to go mingle with other fans and we'd talk to them later. They reluctantly went off to do their own thing, and I hoped that would be the end of them.

Landon and I talked a little more with some fans, I got a few more numbers, and then schmoozed with Micky, trying to get him to book a bunch of reality stars for his bar—always important to network and make all of the connections you can. We heard the bartender scream "Last call!" and I looked at my phone. It was a quarter to two. Where did the night go?

I thanked Micky for everything and told him we'd definitely be in touch. He offered to let us stay past closing hours and party on, but we were both exhausted. "But if you bring in another reality star for an official appearance we'll definitely party after with you guys." Always thinking future business.

Someone from the bar staff drove us back to the hotel, and we went up to our rooms.

"You need to be in the lobby at 8 am for your ride to the airport," I reminded Landon. "Get some sleep!"

"Will do." He shook my hand. "Thanks again for everything, Andy. Awesome doing gigs with you. So much fun."

Yes it was. Such a great night. I walked down the hall to my hotel room, pretty proud of myself for pulling off another successful night, when my phone rang. Pennsylvania area code, not saved in my phone. Who the hell…?

"Andy!" a voice shrieked at me. "It's Jen! We're in the lobby! Let's party!"

Oh shit! I forgot all about annoying Jen and her annoying crew, and that I had told them we can party at the hotel at 2 am. Well, that wasn't going to happen.

"Hey, Jen!" I said, trying to sound happy to hear her voice. "Look, Landon has an early flight tomorrow, so he decided to crash early. I'm gonna do the same. But it was awesome meeting you guys, have a great night!"

Jen would not be brushed off so easily. "Bullshit! We came all the way to the hotel, and we're partying! We'll make Landon wanna party!"

I gave a chuckle. "No, believe me, you won't. He's already asleep."

"We're coming up!"

"You don't even know what floor I'm on."

"Yes I do. I showed the front desk guy your phone number and he matched it to the one on file, so that proved I know you and he gave me your room number. We're on our way now."

"No—"

"We're on our way!" And she hung up.

Fuck! You have to be kidding me. This was a whole new realm for me. I had a crew of drunken girls stalking me. Well, they were stalking me to get to Landon, but still, I was the gatekeeper, and I didn't really know how to handle it. I just wanted to get some sleep.

I was still in the hall mulling my options when Jen and her crew walked out of the elevator. "Okay Andy, shot time!" she shouted when she saw me.

On any other day of my life, if a group of five hot girls stepped out of a hotel elevator demanding to come to my room and do shots, I would have thought I was dreaming. Tonight was different. I already knew these girls, they were obnoxious and impossible to deal with, I was exhausted and Landon was asleep. Plus I knew there'd be many other opportunities for this type of experience, with girls I actually wanted to be with.

I adopted a calm, reasonable persona. "Jen, like I said, I'm sorry. You girls are awesome," I lied, "but we're busy guys and Landon has an early flight tomorrow and I need to drive back to New York. I wasn't thinking when I invited you earlier. My bad. Next time we'll party."

Jen waved my words away. "If you're gonna be a party pooper we'll just go get Landon. He's the one we really wanna see anyway."

"Well, Landon is asleep and I can't give you his room number. So…"

"Already have his room number. It was attached to your reservation. The guy at the front desk showed it to me when he showed me yours."

Shit, we really had some first-class stalkers on our hands. Now the herd started moving; I quickly jumped ahead and tried to corral it. "Girls, like I said, Landon's sleeping. It's rude to wake him up. We'll keep in touch and party with you next time."

They looked at me blankly, completely unmoved by my arguments. "Sorry Andy, we're not leaving without seeing our love Landon."

The girls pushed passed me and headed for Landon's room. When they got there they started banging on the door.

"Laaaannnndonnn, it's us! We wanna see you. Let's do shots and get wild!"

No response.

More door banging. Louder this time.

"Come onnnn Landon. Open up and let us in. We won't disappoint you."

A second later I get a text from Landon: *Dude is that the annoying girls from the bar? Why are they here? Pls get rid of them.*

Me: *I'm trying. They won't leave. They're psychos.*

Landon: *Get hotel security and see if that helps. I'm ignoring them and going to sleep with my headphones on.*

Lucky you.

Louder and constant banging on the door now.

"Landon! What the fuck! Why aren't you opening up? We wanna fuck you so bad. We'll rock your world. Pleeeeease let us fuck you. Pleease!"

Wow—Okay, this needed to stop.

"Listen girls, Landon isn't coming out. He's asleep with his head-phones on and he's not interested. You gotta chill and get out. Now."

"We aren't leaving." I looked at them, with their flashing red eyes and long sharp nails, and I got the sense they would tear me to pieces if I didn't back off. This was not good.

Two hotel security guys came out of the elevator and started walking towards us.

"We've had a complaint of loudness going on out here. What's happening?"

I jumped in quick. "Hi sir. I'm on tour with a reality star and these girls want to see him and they aren't leaving. I told them repeatedly that he isn't interested in hanging out."

"OK, ladies if you don't have a room here you need to leave the hotel immediately," one of the security guys said.

Jen was defiant. "You're a fake cop, we don't have to listen to you."

Oh shit. Here we go.

"Yes you do," said the Security Guy, jabbing a finger at her face, "unless you want the "real" cops here in two minutes hauling you all off to jail. We're escorting you out NOW!"

This was the moment of truth. Would the horny drunk chicks fight or fold? I took a step back. This could get bloody.

After a brief glaring contest, the girls lowered their heads and slowly walked out with security. As they passed me they all gave me the death stare—thanks a lot, asshole. The security guys gave me the stink-eye too. Hey, don't blame me, I just wanted to get some sleep!

Whatever. I never heard from them again. Thankfully. But wow, that was intense.

I booked Landon often after that, but the next time we met up in person was about a year or so later. This time it was a nightclub gig in the "beautiful" city of Poughkeepsie, NY. It was only an hour and a half from Albany, so of course I had to go. The first thing we joked about was those crazy girls from Pennsylvania.

"Let's hope they don't show up," Landon said.

I'd told my good friend Justin how wild these gigs were, so he begged to come with me and experience the Landon phenomenon first-hand. Landon welcomed him aboard: "Any friend of Andy's is a friend of mine."

The club appearance wasn't till midnight (bars in Poughkeepsie can stay open till 4 am), so we had plenty of time to party beforehand. I knew a local college girl named Jackie, who had invited us to her place for a pregame party. The plan was to hit the party, come back to the hotel for more drinks, and then move on to the club gig.

We went to our rooms to shower and iron (as usual), and then we met Landon in the lobby at 9 pm.

"Hey, check these out," said Landon. He pulled out a pile of glossy, full-color postcards, featuring a picture of himself shirtless and smiling, with his name and website on the top.

"Wow, what a beautiful chest," I said drily.

"Help me get these out tonight, will you? I bring them to every gig now. It's all about branding."

Ha! Landon, the master brander. So part of my job tonight would be to put large postcards of a shirtless Landon on the bar counter and tables all around the club, as well as hand them out to everyone in attendance.

"Yeah, these are good to have, in case anyone is like, 'who the hell is this guy?'" I joked. "All they have to do is look at the postcard and they'll know who you are. Of course you might have to take your shirt off for them to recognize you." Landon and Justin laughed.

But his point was not lost on me. Branding is always a good thing. This postcard, comical though it was, served the purpose of getting his website out there, and also gave people something to get signed if they wanted his autograph. It was smart thinking all around.

A minute later my friend Jackie pulled up in a really nice SUV with her attractive friend Courtney. The three of us hopped in and I made the introductions.

"So there's about thirty of us at this pregame party—is that cool? It's mostly girls." Mostly girls? Oh, well. We would survive. "We told some friends Landon was coming, so it got a little bigger than we planned, but we aren't letting anyone else in," Jackie told us.

"Yeah that's cool," I said. "I mean, I don't know how long we'll stay, since we have other stuff going on and we have to be at the club by midnight." I wanted to set up an out for us, since I figured Landon would probably not want to hang too long if it was a small apartment packed with thirty wild fans.

And I was right. We walked in to a mob scene. Drunken college girls, all flocking around Landon. He could barely get a drink. Justin and I were loving the scene, but I didn't want to wear Landon out before the actual event that we were getting paid for. I decided to text another girl I knew from Poughkeepsie, an attractive chick named Caitlin Ryder. She likes to go by Ryder.

Me: *Hey, Ryder, I'm in town with Landon from MTV and we're at some party but looking to leave. You wanna come get some drinks with us at the hotel before we have to be at the club later?*

Ryder: *Hell yeah I'm down. I'm gonna bring my friends Allie and Nicole with me. Is that cool?*

Me: *Yeah definitely, but can you get us from this party and bring us back to the hotel on your way?*

Ryder: *Done. What's the address?*

I got the address from Jackie, and thanked her but told her we had to peace out. It was just too much for Landon and he had to be on his game for the appearance tonight, etc. She said she understood, and that she and her friends would come to the club to party with us later. Worked for me!

Landon, Justin and I went outside to wait for Ryder to show up. When she did, we realized the car was going to be a little cramped. Landon of course sat in front next to Ryder, who was driving. This really short and really cute dark-haired, tan, Italian-looking girl in a tiny dress got out from the back seat to let us in.

"Hi, I'm Nicole! But my friends call me Snooki, so just call me that," she said.

Snooki—strange nickname, I thought. But cool.

That name might ring a bell to you. It should. For me, at this point in time, it didn't. The world famous reality show she was destined to be on was still a few years away.

"Snooki, great to meet you," I said. "This is my friend Justin and I'm sure you know Landon."

She was far more excited to talk to Landon than to me or Justin. "Landon, great to meet you! I'm such a huge fan!"

"Thanks," he said, "Great to meet you too." But I could tell he just wanted to go back to the hotel for some drinks.

I squeezed in first next to Allie, then Justin hopped in. But it wasn't like it was a big back seat. So Justin happily offered to let Snooki sit on his lap. She reluctantly agreed and we went on our way.

As we were slowing down to stop at a traffic light, I noticed out of the corner of my eye Justin putting his arms tightly around Snooki. She quickly turned around and glared at him.

"What the hell are you doing?" Snooki shouted.

"Whoa, Whoa, relax, just helping you out with a human seatbelt so you don't fall forward," Justin responded.

"I don't need a human seatbelt, thank you!" Snooki angrily shot back.

"Okay, okay—sorry!"

I gave Justin a dirty look. He ignored it.

We finished the rest of the ride to the hotel in silence. By the time we got out of the car everything was back to normal and everyone was ready to drink. Landon said he needed just a few minutes to relax so he would have energy for the club appearance. So the rest of us went up to my hotel room to do some shots.

"So—can you cast me on a show?" Snooki asked me as we downed our first two shots.

"I wish," I said. "Unfortunately I don't do casting. But you know, if you ever do get on a show, then I can be your agent and get you paid to do appearances at events around the country. So if you get lucky, let me know."

"I will!" Snooki said.

I was just trying to give her some positive vibes for the future. But I had to admit, she had this fun, outgoing, and extremely unique personality that I thought could work great on a reality show. Who knows, I remember thinking at the time, maybe someday… ?

Allie had more immediate plans. "Do you think I have a chance of hooking up with Landon tonight?"

Already thinking about getting it on with the big reality star. What about me and Justin? The usual story: high hopes, low expectations.

"You never know. But if you want any chance at all, here's my tip: don't be annoying. These girls last year in Pennsylvania were begging Landon for sex. It was pathetic. Just don't do that."

"Of course not," Allie said.

"Can you get us into VIP tonight?" Ryder asked.

"Definitely, VIP and free drinks all night," I said.

We all toasted to a wild Poughkeepsie night ahead. Landon showed up, I poured him a shot, and we toasted again. This time to Landon. Ladies choice. More shots, please! The night was young, the mood was fun, and I was Mr. Reality Star Agent, partying with a celebrity, hot girls, and a good friend along for the ride. Could it get any better?

We arrived at the club by midnight, Landon went to the DJ booth and did his thing, the owner brought a bottle over to our VIP section, and I started pouring. The rest of the night was VERY blurry, but I was assured by my friends the next day that it was off the hook. Translated to today's younger-crowd language: Lit as fuck.

Poughkeepsie was great times, and would end up being a regular spot for me on the reality star touring circuit. In the meantime, it was back to work. As we left Poughkeepsie and said goodbye to Caitlin Ryder and Nicole "Snooki" Polizzi, I never would have imagined that the world would soon know their names.

CHAPTER 5
REALITY LOVE?

RELATIONSHIPS.

The whole business revolves around relationships. Client relationships. Relationships with nightclub and bar owners and promoters, and college events boards. Sponsor relationships. Network relationships.

And then there are Relationship relationships. Love still makes the world go around, and when any group of people spends a lot of time together, bonds form, and romances bloom. It's no different with reality TV. Usually the producers encourage it. What's better for ratings than a secret romance, which turns into a public romance, which hopefully even becomes a broken romance? Talk about a compelling series arc!

I wasn't immune to the allure and the potential windfall of promoting a real-life reality couple. Of course I wanted a piece of it.

At this point I was killing it with the bookings. Gig after gig after gig—I was getting the Z-listers paid for college speeches, nightclub appearances and more. Consequently I was getting more and more clients. The new season of *Real World* had just premiered: *Real World: Austin*. It was a huge hit right off the bat. The entire cast of that show was in crazy demand at the time, and my hope was to work with as many of them as possible.

Two genuine couples emerged from the *Real World: Austin* cast. One was Danny and Melinda; they started dating during the season, and became the big love story of the show. I worked with them a little, but was never really close with them. They ended up getting married, and later divorced.

Wes and Johanna, on the other hand, were more of a foreplay story. They had a sort of tempestuous relationship during the season—he was interested in her, she was dating someone else, he started dating someone else, they made each other jealous and pretended they didn't care—but they never actually came together until after the shoot, so by the time the series hit the air they were a solid couple, and very marketable. When the show's popularity was hitting its peak, I was getting a lot of inquiries about booking them. If only I could!

And that's when I got a call from Wes himself: "Andy—Wes Bergmann, from *Real World: Austin.*"

"Hey Wes! What's up?" I answered with my customary unearned familiarity.

"I got your number from Rachel Robinson, she tells me you handle a lot of reality star bookings."

"That is correct," I said calmly, secretly stoked to hear from him.

"So, you wanna work with me and my girlfriend Johanna? She's also on the show, you know."

Yeah, I kinda knew. Johanna Botta, the gorgeous Peruvian, was high on anybody's radar.

"You know, Wes, that's such a coincidence. I was just thinking about reaching out to you myself. I've been getting a lot of interest in you guys."

"Cool. Well, you have my number, call me whenever you have a potential gig for us…"

"Actually, I already had a club owner ask me about bringing you in. He said $1,000 cash if we can make it happen soon." I figured he's gotta be impressed with my super-immediate results.

"Nope, sorry Andy. I won't do anything less than $1,500. As long as I get that, you can book anything and everything you want."

And that was how it would be from now on with Wes. He was a businessman, through and through. Never taking any less money than he felt he could get.

I called up the club owner and told him we needed $1,500, and if we couldn't get it, there wouldn't be a gig. And he agreed to our terms. It was as simple as that.

I liked this ploy. Establishing a base fee meant I could keep the negotiations to a minimum. And it had the additional advantage of creating a threshold that other cast members wouldn't go below. Thanks to Wes, the top Z-listers pledged an oath to never accept less than that amount of money, no matter what. Which prevented some idiot agent wannabe from peddling a cast member at a fraction of the cost and undercutting my business. And since demand was so high during this time period, I had little problem nabbing bookings. Wes and Johanna each got around two hundred gigs the first year of their show. Big money for barely 21-year-olds.

And because I contributed to getting a good chunk of those gigs, Wes and Johanna and I started getting real close. In fact, we became great friends, and whenever I booked them for a few dates in the northeast, they would use my apartment as home base. Wes and Johanna would fly into Albany, I'd pick them up at the airport, we'd hang out at my place for the night, they'd destroy my couch, and we'd leave the next morning in my car for the gig.

It was during one of these pre-gig nights at my apartment—the three of us sitting in my living room, relaxing with a beer and talking upcoming events—that Wes had one of his many genius business ideas:

"Andy, it's about time we got more money for these nightclub appearances." More money? Sounded good to me. "We gotta spice shit up," he went on.

"Sure—how?"

"You know how these club owners are. They'll do anything to get publicity and fame."

"Kind of like you?" I interjected.

"Basically," said Wes, unfazed. "So here's my thought: we should do a tour where we film a DVD special. We can call it 'Wes and Johanna's Behind the Scenes DVD Filming Nightclub Tour."

I glanced at Johanna, who was just sitting there, amused.

"And who's gonna make this DVD?" I asked.

"We are," Wes responded.

"How are we gonna do that?"

"It's simple: the three of us split the cost of a cool profession-al-looking video camera; then you tell the nightclubs we're filming an upcoming DVD during the entire tour, and we'll include their venue name on the DVD."

Sounded a little sketchy to me, and Wes noticed my skepticism.

"You'll be featured in the video too!" he quickly added. "The DVD is all about life on tour with us, and you're on tour, you're the agent, so…if you want to create a comprehensive picture, you gotta include agent—you!"

The wily Wes was playing to my not-so-secret wish to be a reality star myself. He intuited—quite correctly—that the promise of a little camera-time would entice me to buy into his scheme.

But I wasn't sold yet. "OK, so who would do the filming?"

"Bring one of your friends along. Tell them it's free drinks and plenty of ladies to go around if they film us for a few hours each night."

Hmm. Maybe it would work. Out of curiosity we looked up some professional cameras online and found an amazing one on sale for $2,100.

"That's only $700 each," Wes said. "Minimal investment for maximum return. Johanna, are you in?"

I expected Johanna to put the kibosh on it, but she threw it back to me. "Andy, what do you think? Can you get us a lot of gigs for more money with this plan?"

"I mean…it's possible. I couldn't guarantee anything. But are you saying you're open to it?" Johanna was usually the more rational one of the two.

"It's only $700, I think it's worth a shot," she responded.

Well, that was two votes in favor. But they couldn't do it without me, so Wes stared at me expectantly with a mischievous grin on his face.

"Andy???" he asked.

"Ugh, fine, we'll give it a try. But you guys make WAY more

than I do, so whether this works out or not, I'm keeping the camera. Deal?"

"Deal," they both agreed.

With the verbal agreement in place, Wes wasted no time ordering the camera online and having it delivered to me. By the time we got back from our gigs that weekend, it had already arrived at my place. I had to admit, it looked really professional and was a cool ass camera. I was getting a Spielberg vibe just holding it.

I drove Wes and Johanna to the airport and as soon as I got back to my place I started making calls pitching the DVD tour. And holy shit, Wes was right! I was able to get over twice as much as a normal appearance. And it wasn't just a date or two. By the end of the day I had strung together a two-week tour. The cost of the video camera was paid for many times over. As, of course, Wes predicted.

We were all thrilled about the two-week tour and the big money it would bring in. It was scheduled for early May, two months away, and I still had to get someone to do the filming. I knew just who to call.

I first met Mario Nacev when he owned a pizza place next door to my apartment in Albany. He was in his early/mid-20s like me, and all about making money, and meeting girls, also like me. Unlike me he stood at a dominating 6'4" and weighed in at 300 pounds.

His pizza place was called Raffaele's, and it was known as THE late night pizza spot. All of the college kids would go there after the bars closed at 4 am to get their drunk bellies filled. Raffaele's didn't even open until evening: the hours were 6 pm through 5 am. I'd stop there all the time late at night for a slice, and joke with Mario about all of the hotties trying out his pizza. And once I heard about his special house rule, known as Smitty's Law, I knew this guy would become a good friend.

"Smitty's Law is in full effect, Andy," Mario said to me the third or fourth time I came into his place.

"What's Smitty's Law?" I asked.

"Come back for a drink and I'll explain."

Raffaele's didn't sell alcohol, but Mario did have a keg of beer in the back room next to the dough maker for him and his friends to enjoy. He poured me a glass and sat back to explain.

"My buddy Smitty came up with this idea when I first opened last year, and I loved it so much that I named it after him. Basically, if a girl comes in and flashes her tits, she gets a free slice of pizza."

"Are you serious!?" I enthusiastically asked.

Mario nodded. "The word's really getting around, and all the girls know about it. So they're ready to flash as soon as they come in. They get pizza, I get bobos" ("bobos" being Mario's pet name for female breasts). "It's a win-win."

"Just a plain slice?"

"No, any style they want. Pepperoni, sausage, the works. Hey, they want to show me the rack, I'm not gonna nickel-and-dime them."

"That's awesome."

"Just hang out in here for more than ten minutes and you'll see."

So I did. And damned if it wasn't true. This hot chick walks in, Mario says "Can I help you?" she lifts up her shirt and Boom!—free slice.

So Raffaele's became my new hang-out, so to speak. I'd head over around 3 am after a night out, go behind the counter, and serve pizza for an hour or so, just to see how many tits I could glimpse each night. Mario liked the free help during the busy time, and I liked the floor show. On an average weekend night we'd give out about 30 free slices before closing time. No wonder he eventually went out of business.

So our friendship blossomed. Mario was constantly asking me about my job. He was so intrigued.

"You're telling me you go to these reality-star events and there's girls everywhere?"

"Picture late night at Raffaele's multiplied by a hundred."

Mario was salivating. "You gotta bring me to that shit, man."

"Sure" I said. "Eventually."

Eventually finally came when we needed a cameraman. One day as I was working out the logistics for the upcoming "Wes and Johanna Behind the Scenes DVD Filming Nightclub Tour" I walked over to Raffele's at 6 pm, just as Mario was opening for the night. It was the earliest I had ever set foot in the place.

"Mario! What's up dude?" I yelled as I saw him putting his first pizza into the oven.

"Andy, what the hell are you doing here so early?"

"I wanted to catch you while I'm sober, and before the craziness begins. I got a great opportunity for you. I'm doing a two-week tour with two reality stars from MTV—Johanna and Wes—and we're bringing a video camera to film the whole thing. We need a camera guy." I could see Mario's eyes getting bigger and bigger. "There's no pay, and you'd be sharing a hotel room with me, but the drinks are free and the girls will be endless. You want in?"

"100% in, yes yes and yes," Mario excitedly responded. "What are the dates?"

"First two weeks of May."

"Can't fucking wait!"

And so it was set. The tour was booked, we had our cameraman, and the deposits were already rolling in. Thousands here, thousands there—it was nuts. There were both college gigs and nightclub gigs on the tour, and I was able to work it out so the first date on the tour was at a community college right near Albany. As usual Wes and Johanna would fly in and stay at my place the night before the gig, then head over to the event the next day.

Things didn't start as smoothly as I'd hoped. As soon as I picked them up at the airport, Wes and Johanna were yelling at each other—something to do with the house they'd bought together in Arizona (which didn't make sense to me anyway— barely 21 and they're already buying a house together—I didn't approve, but it wasn't my place to say). Wes hopped in the front seat and Johanna got in the back, and they were off to the races.

"You're so fucking annoying, Wes," Johanna yelled at him.

"Can you just relax?" Wes replied.

"No, I can't relax! And I can't believe I have to do this fucking tour with you for two fucking weeks! Fuck this."

Gonna be a looong trip.

But if one minute they'd be bitching and sniping, the next minute they'd be all over each other. By the time we arrived at my apartment the mood had done a complete 180.

"Wesy-poo, I love you," Johanna said, kissing him as they got out of the car.

"I love you too, baby."

It was clear to me that, even in the "reality" world, love could actually be genuine. This was not a made-up relationship for TV. It was the real deal. And while I was the constant third wheel in their fighting-and-loving scenario, it sure as hell was entertaining.

And to be honest, I didn't really feel like a third wheel. Wes and Johanna treated me like we'd been friends for years. The fact that I was making them a shitload of money helped, but nevertheless, we got along great. They never once complained about sleeping on my disgusting old living room couch, a hand-me down from my aunt. And as long as the hotels on the road were good, we were good.

After they got settled in, I broke out some beers and we went over the itinerary for the tour. Some highlights included: a Voter Registration Awareness event first, then a five-hour drive out to Buffalo the day after for a nightclub gig; then an eight-hour drive to NJ for a "behind the scenes of reality TV" college speech, followed by a nightclub later that night about 30 minutes away; a three-hour drive to another college gig on Alcohol Awareness in Reading, PA, which we were told would be mandatory for all students in fraternities and sororities to attend; finally a five-hour drive to a nightclub appearance in New Haven, CT. So yeah, maybe this tour wasn't routed as neatly as Taylor Swift's team would plan it, but I did the best I could with the offers and dates we got. We were all prepared for a lot of driving.

After several drinks deep it was getting late, and I wanted to have energy for the first tour gig tomorrow. "Okay guys, I'm gonna get some sleep. Help yourself to any more drinks or food or whatever. Need anything else out here?" I asked.

"Nah, we're set," Wes replied. "We might be a little loud though—just an FYI."

And FYI, they were. Very loud. They were having a great time on my dirty old couch, making noises I'd never heard before. Fortunately I had my trusty window air conditioner and it was a warm early May night, so I blasted that on high and the noise mostly drowned them out.

I got up early the next morning to beat them to the shower. By the time Wes and Johanna woke up I was ready to go. They showered together to save time, and just as they were done getting ready the door buzzed. I looked out the window and saw Mario's towering frame waiting at the door. I buzzed him in and introduced him to Wes and Johanna.

"Great to meet you guys," Mario said. "So excited to be part of this."

"Mario! You should be our security, you're huge as fuck," Wes said jokingly.

"I can do that too. I'm a man of many talents," Mario replied.

Wes and I gave Mario a quick overview of how to use the video camera, and he figured it all out and more pretty quickly. Then we piled in my car, Mario in front due to his size, and went off to the college.

We arrived around 10:30 am for the 11 am gig. It was the end of the semester and Wes and Johanna had been booked to help with voter registration. The college hoped that by having two famous reality stars hang out in the main quad, students would come over to meet them and then register to vote. It was all taking place during the no-class block from 11am to 1pm, when the quad would be busiest.

I had already discussed crowd control and logistics with the student activities advisor when we were writing up the contract. Having seen time and time again how these Z-listers bring in the huge crowds, especially college students, I knew it was best to be prepared. It could turn out to be a mob scene.

Or not.

We arrived at the quad. There was no dressing room for us, no drinks, no food.

And no fans.

There were, however, three well-dressed official-looking students standing alone by the voter registration table. The Student Advisor, Jim, shook my hand. "You must be Andy," He introduced me to Angie and Kara, the student leaders who were hoping to rock the vote. "Listen, not sure why it's slow today, I think a lot of students are skipping class and didn't come to campus." Like most community colleges it was a commuter school, so the students generally drove in. Or didn't.

"Well, we'll make the most of it," I said.

"Yeah, we're here for you, so whatever you need us to do, we'll do," Wes said brightly.

"Yeah," Johanna added with less enthusiasm. I could see from her face that she was already having second thoughts about this grand money-making bonanza.

Mario was getting the whole exciting exchange on film. He even had "release forms" for those on camera to sign, to make it seem very legit.

"Since it's still slow out here," Angie said, "here's some meal tickets if you guys wanna get an early lunch in the dining hall."

The dining hall! And Landon complained about Applebee's! But you always have to put on a professional demeanor when you're getting paid, that was the lesson Veronica and Rachel taught me that really stuck.

"Thanks so much Angie, we appreciate it," I said. I caught Johanna rolling her eyes next to me.

We walked over to the dining hall alone. Mario was still filming. "You can cut for now," I told him.

They were changing over from breakfast to lunch when we arrived, so we had a combination of cold bacon, rubbery scrambled eggs, dry hard sausage, and a salad from the salad bar. Awesome stuff. But that was the deal with reality star tours: sometimes it was a five-star Italian restaurant, sometimes it was Applebee's, and sometimes it was the campus dining hall. You win some, you lose some.

After savoring our "meal", we went back over to the quad. The college had an area set up for Wes and Johanna next to the voter registration table. Jim gave them a wireless mic. "There are speakers set up on the quad. Maybe you can try to get more people to come over?"

"Sure!" Johanna took the mic: "Come on over and register to vote and get a picture with me and Wes while you do!" she shouted.

Three students answered the call and came over.

Before things could get any worse, I reminded Jim that we weren't paid yet. He promptly handed me the college issued check for $7,500. Divided up that would be $3,000 for Wes, $3,000 for Johanna, $1,500 for me. Not a bad take for hanging outside on a college campus for a few hours. Even if it was kind of embarrassing for Wes and Johanna.

"Andy, this is annoying. We're just standing here, no one gives a shit," Wes said.

"Just chill out, we got paid," I waved the check at him. "It's only for another hour. You're a big boy, you can handle it," I said.

A few more students showed up before 1, and in the end about 50 in total registered to vote at the event.

"This was a big success in the eyes of the college," Advisor Jim assured us.

As we walked back to the car, trying to enjoy our dubious success, Mario came up alongside me. "So Andy, this isn't exactly what I pictured when you told me about your amazing reality star events."

I had to laugh. "Ha—yeah, sorry man, this was not a typical gig. But you never know with reality stars. People love them or hate them or don't even know them."

"Nobody hates us," Wes chimed in.

Sure buddy.

"Next gig I'm sure will be better," Johanna said.

And it was.

IN FACT THE REST OF THE tour went out off without a hitch for the most part. The biggest hurdle for me was the room accommodations. The first night on the road, I learned that sharing a room with my pizza pal Mario was going to be absolute torture. Oh, he was good company while he was awake, but when it came time to crash, he was out like a light, and within a matter of seconds the guy was snoring louder than I had ever heard before, producing noises that seemed hardly human. And whenever he subsided and I didn't hear anything for a minute or so and was about to drift off myself, out of nowhere I'd be jolted awake by an explosive snore louder than any before, as if he'd been saving up all the smaller snores in those quiet moments and then shot them out all at once in one great blast. It was like a race car engine revving up, no exaggeration.

I couldn't win—if it wasn't Wes and Johanna bonking, it was Mario honking. Anyway, I got no sleep that night, and the next day I made sure to get some headphones so I could shut out the unrelenting assault. To this day I dread those rare occasions when we still have to share a room.

But I had to adapt, because Mario was here to stay. After he got to experience his share of successful gigs, he was hooked. The whole car ride of the tour, from Pennsylvania to Connecticut, he wouldn't shut up about how amazing it was.

"I love how you guys hype up the crowd behind the DJ booth, and pour shots in the mouths of everyone while you're standing on the bar. That's so great. And the bobos! I love all the bobos!"

"Bobos?" asked Johanna from the back.

"Never mind," I told her.

We were heading to the last stop of the tour now—Club Alchemy in New Haven—and Mario suggested we spice things up a little. "You know what you should do? Contests. This is a big nightclub, right, so you get the audience members on stage and have a contest. It'll be fun to film that shit, and the crowd would love it," exclaimed Mario.

"Cool idea, but what kind of contest?" I asked.

"You know—adult stuff. Sexy. Risqué." He surprised me with the fancy word.

"Like what?"

"I don't know." Mario is the master of ideas, but he's a little lacking in the elaboration-and-follow-through department.

"I have some ideas," Johanna piped up from the back seat. She went on to tell us about two different contests that she saw at an event once.

The first one: You get an equal number of guys and girls from the crowd. Pair them up randomly with the opposite sex. Each guy gets an open full bottle of beer. Each girl gets down on her knees next to her partner. The guy puts the bottle in between his thighs.

When the host says GO, the girls have to suck the beer out of the bottle while it's between their partners legs. Whoever empties the bottle first wins.

Not exactly *Jeopardy*, but you couldn't deny the visual appeal.

"Hilarious!" Mario said. "Let's do it, that'll make great video footage." Wes and I agreed that it would be funny as hell.

"But hold on," said Johanna. "If you guys like that idea, you'll love this one."

The second contest started the same way: you gather an equal number of guys and girls from the crowd. Since this contest is pretty racy, you could invite couples to come up together if they wanted, or pair people up randomly if they're comfortable with that. Because basically it was a Sexual Position contest. One "couple" would take the stage at a time, and the DJ would play a dance song. The goal is for the couple to get into sexual positions, the wilder and crazier the better, doing poses, dance moves, gyrations, etc. while the music plays. The frenzy of the crowd response determines the winner.

"I vote for that contest," I said.

"Definitely!" agreed Mario.

"I'll leave it up to you guys," Wes said, being the ever well-behaved boyfriend. "As long as the club is okay with it."

"The owner sounded pretty cool, so I think they will be," I replied.

We arrived at the hotel, and fortunately our rooms were ready. I had stipulated three rooms in this contract so that Mario and I wouldn't have to share. No obnoxious snoring for me tonight.

The club wasn't taking us out to dinner, but it did offer an extra $40 per person to cover dinner costs. We pocketed the money and ate light. Then we got ready for the 10:30 pm hotel lobby pickup. The club owner had texted me that they were already at capacity of 2,000 people and the line was a few blocks long, so Mario and I were already starting to celebrate.

"Now *this* is what I was talking about," I told him as we did a shot in my hotel room.

"Can't wait man. I want some bobos tonight."

Wes and Johanna were waiting for us in the lobby, and our

ride to the club pulled up in front a few minutes later—it was a vintage 1995 Toyota Corolla. Not sure who used it before us, but there were about a dozen bags of old McDonald's and Burger King wrappers all over the seats.

"Sorry about the mess," the scrawny driver said to us. "I didn't know until five minutes ago that I had to pick you guys up."

We said nothing. Just wanted to get to the club and out of this car as fast as possible. Johanna in particular, in her short tight dress, was not loving the sensation of sitting between a Whopper wrapper and a McNugget container.

The owner, Dewy, met us outside of Club Alchemy in downtown New Haven. "Great to meet you guys!" he said.

It wasn't worth complaining to him about the shitty ride from the hotel. The hotel was nice, the club was packed, and he'd already agreed to the Sexual Position contest, so why make waves?

We were ushered directly to the DJ booth. The DJ stopped the music and got on the mic.

"New Haven! Guess who's here?! Please give a loud ass Connecticut welcome to Wes and Johanna from *MTV's Real World Austin*!"

As the crowd cheered, Wes got on the mic and started cranking them up.

"I say 'New', you say 'Haven'. NEW!"

"HAVEN!" the crowd of fans screamed.

"I say 'Club', you say 'Alchemy'. CLUB!"

"ALCHEMY!" the crowd screamed again.

"We're here to party with you guys ALL NIGHT!" Johanna yelled.

The crowd went crazy, and Dewy brought us all over to the VIP area, with Mario filming the action for our "DVD."

While we did the usual routine- pouring drinks, flirting with girls, taking pictures of fans with the reality stars—Dewy handed me the remaining half of our $5,000 fee, which was huge for a nightclub appearance. I wasn't thrilled about having $2,500 cash in my pocket the rest of the night while drinking, but it came with the territory. The struggle is real.

We weren't asked to do much, just hang out in VIP and mingle with the fans. But about an hour before closing Dewy came back over to me.

"Andy—what about that contest you promised us?"

"Oh yeah! The contest!" I called over to Wes and Johanna, "You guys ready for the Sexual Position contest?"

"Let's do it," Johanna said.

Dewy brought us to the big stage in the club. Johanna got on the mic. "Okay, we're going to have a very special contest, and we need five guys and five girls. Couples are welcome. Come on up!" Johanna said to the crowd.

In less than a minute we had our ten contestants. After I helped them on stage, Johanna explained the concept. "This is called the Sexual Position Contest," she said, as a wave of laughter swept through the audience. We figured that if you explained the idea beforehand, we might get only the completely-shit-faced drunk-off-their-asses couples involved. This way, once we got them on stage, there was much less chance of them backing out.

As it happened, one pair did drop out immediately. They were buzzed, but not *that* buzzed. Still, four pairs were game, and that was plenty.

"Okay, Mr. DJ, let's start the music for couple number 1," Wes shouted.

Andy filming the crowd while Johanna pours shots at an event

The music blared, and Couple No. 1, who had just met two minutes earlier, started going at it. The girl had on a tiny skirt that was showing off basically everything. The guy was throwing her this way and that way, tossing her and spinning her and dry-humping her on stage. The crowd cheered in encouragement, my man Mario screaming the loudest. Eventually, as the guy was thrusting into her a little too energetically from behind, her "bobos" popped out. The place exploded. Mario was in heaven.

Repeat that routine three more times, and you'll have a mild idea of the high-octane depravity we were providing the good customers of Club Alchemy. It was wild, insane, everything you might expect from spring break in Cancun, not a nightclub in New Haven. The crowd was deafeningly loud, and the contest just blew the roof off the place. The 2,000 fans in the venue loved it, and nobody more so than Mario.

"Well, Andy, I got my bobos." He said, a look of blissful satisfaction on his face. "This was everything you promised, and more. Thanks again, man."

"Hey, thank *you*. We couldn't have done this filming thing without you. Not sure who I would've trusted to come along with us and do it for free."

"Not exactly free. I'm getting booze, food, and girls. Who needs money?" Mario said.

I did. I saw his point, but for me you had to include money in the equation. You gotta get paid.

Still, I admit, I was loving every second of it. Sure, some gigs had their downsides—lower turnouts, shitty food, disgusting car rides. But these were Z-listers, and for each downside there were twenty more upsides. So keep them coming!

CHAPTER 6
POST REALITY LOVE

WES AND JOHANNA WERE A COUPLE for the ages. They were young, they were beautiful, and they were born to be on camera. Their fans adored them, the infotainment shows featured them constantly, and best of all, in a world of fake reality, their romance was real. They were madly in love with each other. I could attest to that, having witnessed first-hand the fighting and the making-up, and the wearing out of my couch. And since their romance began on reality TV, what better way to seal the deal than by getting married in a reality TV wedding extravaganza? It would complete the arc of their television saga, and be the perfect beginning to a great life together, and hopefully a whole new series. Their love would surely stand the test of time.

Until it didn't. Suddenly Wes and Johanna were over. Which sadly is in the nature of reality romances. Neither of them was on a show that was currently airing, people stopped talking about them, and without that ready-made publicity the general interest in their romance waned considerably. When the spotlight disappeared, so did their main reason for staying together. The relationship fizzled, and so did my 20% commission.

But life goes on. And in the settlement of their break-up, I got custody of Wes.

Johanna and I continued working together at first, but our interests diverged and the gigs were less and less. With Wes it was just the opposite. We became closer, and I started booking him as a single man all over the country. Wes continued to appear on new seasons of *The Challenge*, and demand for him wasn't decreasing at all. I'd get call after call from nightclubs, wanting to book him for an appearance. The money kept rolling in, which was one of the things that cemented our relationship. We were both very fond of the green stuff. We also bonded over our mutual desire for hot girls at the events (something he was not interested in during his ultra-loyal boyfriend days with Johanna).

Of course I had other clients who needed my attention, but Wes was smart. He knew how to focus me on getting him gigs over the other reality star "competitors."

So when I saw "WesMTV" come up on my caller ID, I was pretty sure he had another idea cooking. "Andy!" Wes said, "MTV is flying me to New York City to film a *Challenge* Reunion episode next month. How about you book me for some appearances within driving distance of NYC for that weekend?"

"What do you consider 'driving distance'?" I asked, immediately alert to the practicality of getting him from the city to an outside gig.

"You know, Albany, Philadelphia, whatever."

"Yeah—who's doing the driving?" I asked skeptically.

"No worries. MTV says they'll foot the bill for a flight anywhere, as long as we can make it into the city in time for the shoot. You can handle driving me into the city right, Andy? You're a big boy. Plus," he added, saving the biggest selling point for last, "since you're gonna be hanging with me, my main goal and mission of the weekend will be to get you laid."

Okay, now he had my attention. "Oh really?"

"Yes really. It is going to happen."

"I'm sold," I responded.

So I went to work and tried to line up some gigs. The film shoot was set to take place on a Saturday morning at the MTV studios in Time Square. Wes had an 8 am call time, and filming would last all day.

The plan would be for Wes to fly into Albany on Friday, do a gig in my hometown, then I'd get him down to New York City by 8 am the next morning. After the filming we'd leave the city and drive to an appearance at a bar in Connecticut, somewhere about an hour away from Hartford. I found this place on a Google search of Connecticut bars and figured I'd give them a call to see if they had interest. They did, and it was set. Sometimes it was that simple.

The Albany gig, which should have been the easy part, took a little more convincing on my part to make happen. I really wanted to do Albany, just for the chance to show my hometown friends just how amazing these reality star appearances were. And there was one place I specifically wanted to book: the hottest, wildest, busiest place in downtown Albany, the Pearl Street Pub.

Known as PSP, the Pearl Street Pub is owned by my good friend Chris Pratt. Not Chris Pratt the movie star (although he does have a cameo in a movie, and owns property that has been used for movie sets). The Albany Chris Pratt is a 50-year-old bald guy. But that's not doing him justice, because this 50-year-old bald guy looks younger than almost any 30-year-old with a full head of hair. I like to refer to him as the King of Albany; he owns several bars and restaurants, but PSP is the one nightclub in his repertoire. Chris is the type of owner that is hands-on. On any given Saturday night, you'll find him behind the bar, playing the music himself for the 2,000 or more club goers at his venue. He definitely knows the importance of being involved and making sure the customers get what they want.

So I figured booking Wes at PSP would be an easy sell. When I stopped down to discuss it with Chris, he was just heading over to Public House 42, one of his other joints, to take care of a few things. "Hey Andy—I only have a minute."

I had to make this quick. "So I have Wes Bergmann, one of the biggest stars from MTV's *Real World* and *The Challenge*?—he's coming through the area in a few weeks and I'd love to bring him to PSP."

"Sure, bring him in, I'll hook you guys up with a few drinks."

"No, he gets paid to come to clubs."

"He gets *paid*?" I'd heard this response before, and it didn't bode well.

"Sure, that's what my business is all about. I've told you this before."

"I guess I wasn't listening."

Time for the hard sell. "See, you promote his appearance here, and since he has millions of fans, so many extra people will come out that night to meet him, you'll pack the place."

"I already pack the place. Besides, I have no idea who he is."

"Wes Bergmann, Chris! *Real World*!"

It meant nothing to Chris, and he let me know it with an indifferent shrug. The hot bartender standing nearby was listening in, and I could see that she knew exactly who I was talking about. Too bad she wasn't hiring.

'How much does this guy want?" asked Chris.

"He normally gets at least $1,500, but since he's going through the area anyway, I can do it for $1,200."

Chris scoffed. "Way too much for some idiot reality star. No thanks."

He was ready to walk away when the hot bartender jumped in, just in the nick of time.

"Chris! Come on, it's Wes from *Real World*. I lovvvvve Wes!"

"Really?" said Chris. "You've heard of this big 'star'?"

'Of course!" she said. "All my girls have, too. Just do it, it'll be worth it, I promise!" I loved this girl, I wanted to kiss her. I wanted to do a lot of things to her, truth be told.

Chris was still pondering. "So you really think I should do it?"

"Yes!" she enthused. "Definitely!"

Chris shrugged again, this time in surrender. "You're lucky she was here, Andy. I'm gonna trust her and give it a try. Send me this superstar's pics so I can post about it on Facebook."

"Awesome, Chris, will do. Thanks—looking forward to it!"

I got out of there quick before he could change his mind, and texted Wes that we were good to go. "*Don't forget your mission,*" I reminded him.

The big weekend came and I picked Wes up from the airport. He was a little wistful and nostalgic in the car. "It's weird coming here without Johanna," he said.

I wasn't in the mood to go down memory lane. "Are you gonna be mopey all weekend?" I asked him.

"Not unless you're a little bitch—then I'll complain about everything."

He wasn't joking.

But it wasn't until we got back to my place and started going over the details of the weekend that the complaining started. And I was the one who was doing it: "So you have to be at the filming in NYC at 8 am tomorrow?"

"Yeah, I told you, man. Can't be late."

"Shit, it takes like two and a half hours to get to the city, and we gotta leave time to stop at your hotel and then walk over to the studio," I said, working it out in my head. "That means we have to basically leave right from the bar when it closes at 4 am."

"We gotta do what we gotta do," Wes said flatly.

"But that means I can't drink at all! I have to drive right from the club all the way down to NYC!" It's important to keep in mind that for a 20-something like myself on a Friday night, drinking was just slightly less essential to one's social health than breathing.

"That's part of the agent's job," said Wes. "That's why you get the big bucks."

"Funny," I said, unamused. "This really sucks."

Wes was unmoved by my plight. "Deal with it, Andy. You knew the plan before this weekend. Don't worry, you can get drunk tomorrow night in Connecticut."

"Or YOU can drive my car from Albany to the city."

"I'm the talent. You drive me."

He was right, of course, but he was also pulling rank on me, and it pissed me off a little. *"Sure, I'll be your chauffeur, Mr. Z-lister."* I didn't actually say this, but I thought it pretty loud.

"Don't worry," Wes added, "you can sleep in my hotel in Times Square while I go to the studio."

It was fine, of course, I was still making a few hundred and I'd get to hang out with my friends later. But that drive down would definitely suck.

I packed up my stuff so it was all ready to go, and we went out to dinner with a few of my friends who had begged to meet Wes. Then it was time to head over to the club.

I texted Chris: *On our way over.*

Chris: *I'll meet you out front, the line is already an hour wait to get in.*

Me: *Perfect!*

Chris wasn't lying. The line outside was insane. People saw Wes walking up and they started shouting his name. I could tell Chris was surprised at how many fans Wes had.

"Well Andy, you were right," he said.

I loved hearing that.

We walked into PSP, and found thousands of fans waiting for Wes. The club has two floors, and the main level, painted in deep red, has a huge bar to the left side and an area in the middle where people can dance to old school hits.

We followed Chris up the back private stairway to the nightclub level on the second floor. There must have been over a thousand people in there dancing to the music. We went over to the DJ booth, Wes said hi to the cheering crowd, and then Chris brought us over to our VIP booth area where bottles were waiting as usual. Wes poured himself a drink, and then poured me one.

"Oops, never mind, none for you," he said mockingly, and pulled the drink away.

"Asshole," I grumbled.

"You're not drinking?" Chris asked.

"I have to drive Wes down to NYC right after we're done."

"That sucks," Chris said.

Exactly. But business is business.

The night actually went off without a hitch. It was a typical nightclub appearance, except for the fact that I didn't have a drink in my hand. Which changed my perspective considerably. I couldn't wait for the gig to be over.

In the meantime, girls were flocking to Wes, and he was talking me up. "Ladies, meet my agent Andy," he'd say to every group of girls that came over.

"Do you know how much money this guy has made me over the last year?"

"How much?" they'd respond.

"5 million dollars!" he very much over-exaggerated.

"Ohhh that's so cool. Andy, take my number…"

Numbers weren't going to do me any good tonight. As I reminded Wes, there would be no after parties. "Thanks for thinking of me, dude, but we're heading out of town as soon as we leave the building."

"I know, I'm just practicing my routine," he said. "I want to make sure you're taken care of tomorrow night. That's my mission."

Chris brought Wes up onto the bar and they both poured shots into the mouths of thirsty club-goers. My friends loved it. I got them into VIP with us and made sure they got some free drinks. Now the nay-sayers were finally understanding the allure of the agent life-style.

As the night was winding down, Chris brought me back to his office to pay me the cash he owed.

"Thanks Chris," I said as I counted the money. "I hope we can do this again with you."

"Absolutely, man. Wes is great to work with, and the fan base is obviously there. Definitely down to do more soon."

Awesome. Chris can be a tough businessman, but you have to be tough to be successful. At least he gave my idea a chance (thanks to that hot bartender), and he would work with me on many gigs after that. So if you ever find yourself in downtown Albany, make sure you check out the hottest club in the city, Pearl Street Pub, and say hi to Chris. You can't miss him—he'll be either standing behind the bar playing the music, or standing on the bar pouring a shot into your mouth.

Wes was definitely tipsy when we hopped in the car at 4 am to head down to the city.

"I'm gonna pass out for the drive, okay?" he asked.

"Yeah, whatever," I responded with annoyance.

Andy and Wes having a quick a beer on the way to their next tour stop

As I drove south on the Thruway, I was thinking that I really needed to count my blessings. So I couldn't drink, and I had to drive in the middle of the night—still, how cool was it that I had just done a paid event with my reality star friend, and was driving to NYC so he could film an MTV reunion special in Times Square, and then would go to another event that night, where I'd get paid to party again? Life wasn't so bad, was it?

About halfway down to the city I had about a gallon of gas left in the tank so I stopped at a service area to fill up. As I was pumping the gas, Wes woke up and got out of the car and lit a bowl. Now that he was a single man, he was partying more, drinking more, and smoking more weed. I had no objections to this on philosophical grounds, but in light of the fact that we were in the middle of a gas station, it seemed just a little risky.

"Dude, I don't think you should be smoking at a rest stop, let alone right next to the gas pump," I yelled at him.

"It's fine, relax." He took a hit. "Want some?"

I declined. Typical Wes, he lived a charmed life, so he assumed he could get away with anything. And he usually did.

While I was grumbling to myself, about thirty seconds later a loud voice came over the speakers:

"THERE IS NO SMOKING AT THE GAS PUMPS. PUT IT OUT IMMEDIATELY," the voice thundered out like the voice of God.

"Told you dude."

Wes put it out, hopped back in the car, and went back to sleep.

Fortunately, there was very little traffic driving down to the city in the pre-dawn hours. We zipped through the Lincoln Tunnel in record time and pulled right up to the hotel in Time Square, where I handed my keys to the valet.

Then I had second thoughts. "Wes, this is being charged to the room, right? MTV better be paying for this," I said.

"Don't worry, they are." Wes was always saying 'don't worry'. It worried me.

We got into our hotel room just before 7 am. Wes jumped in the shower and I passed out on the big king bed.

An hour later Wes was poking me. "Andy, I'm outta here."

"Have fun filming," I said half asleep.

"Your name will be at the front, just come over when you're up. We're filming until 5."

"Thanks."

I slept for another much-needed six hours and then got up and headed over to the MTV studios.

"Andy Binder, here for *The Challenge* Reunion taping," I said to the security guy in front.

"The audience was let in hours ago. You're too late," he rudely responded.

I know, I wanted to say, because I just woke up after driving all the way from fucking Albany. But I stayed cool. "I'm not part of the audience," I explained. "I'm an agent of one of the reality stars being filmed today. He told me I'd be on the list and I can get in whenever."

"You're on the list?" he said with a sarcastic smirk.

"Yes, I'm on the list."

The security guy checked again.

"Okay, you're on the list. Go ahead in." As I breezed past him, he needed to assert his tiny authority one more time. "Don't walk into the studio when the red light is on."

Yeah, I knew all about the red light. I walked up the stairs and into the legendary MTV Times Square studios. This was where MTV's *Total Request Live* with Carson Daly was filmed for years. The *TRL* second floor studio famously had windows that overlooked Times Square, and thousands of fans used to hang out on the street hoping to catch a glimpse of their favorite stars.

I felt like I was walking through history as I strolled down the MTV hallway and looked at the countless pictures of huge superstars who had graced those same halls with their presence. There was little fanfare today, and the famous studio windows were covered. But there was still a nice little audience of hardcore *Challenge* fans inside, eager to see their favorite stars from the show reunite and gossip and yell at each other. At the end of every *Challenge* season, MTV invites the top cast members back to be interviewed and to hash out all of their differences and stir up even more drama. The fans couldn't get enough.

As I walked on set, Wes gave me a nod, and I hung out in the back to watch. And watch, and watch. The reunion would air as an hour special, but damn it took long to film. They'd do question after question, take after take. I got there at around 2 pm and those three remaining hours of filming felt like an eternity. It was cool to observe, once, but I didn't feel any need to go back, ever.

When it was finally a wrap, I went up to Wes, and said hi to some of the other cast members who I knew or who I wanted to know. And then we had to go. It was a three-hour ride to our next gig, and we needed some time beforehand to get ready and relax and have a few drinks. I was definitely having a few drinks tonight.

"Damn, that was miserable," Wes said as we left the studios.

"Yeah, tough life of fame," I said.

"You try sitting up there for eight hours with no sleep, having to be on your game for national TV."

"Better than driving at 4 am from Albany to New York City." I wasn't letting go of that grievance just yet.

We both surprisingly had a lot of energy on the ride to Connecticut. I was looking forward to actually being able to drink tonight, and Wes just seemed glad to not have to deal with the filming anymore. "And don't forget—the mission," I reminded him.

"I didn't forget," he said, and proceeded to outline his rating system. "It's my Area Code Girl Rating System." I was intrigued, and he went on to explain:

"Area codes have 3 numbers. So do girls. The first number, from 0 to 9, is based on the girl's face. 0 is the ugliest face possible, 9 is the hottest. The second number can only be either 0 or 1. 0, you'd never fuck her in a million years, and 1, you would. Simple. And the third number is her body: 0 it's a terrible body and 9 it's the best body you could ever imagine."

"So, the best possible girl is a 919?" I asked.

"You got it. And the beauty of this system is it's all in code, we can use it in front of everybody and no one will know what the fuck we're talking about."

"Anyway—remember your mission. She better be at least a 717," I said.

"I'm thinking you should be happy with a 516," Wes said.

"I'll compromise with a 617."

"Don't be surprised if you wind up with a 414," Wes joked.

"I don't think a 414 would exist for me. More like a 404," I said.

"Beggars can't be choosers, dude."

"Shut up, Wes." I got to thinking. "I wonder how many 000s there will be tonight."

"Hopefully none."

We got to the hotel (well, it was more like a motel) in the middle of nowhere Connecticut around 9 pm. Good timing since we had an hour or so to change and get ready and have a few drinks. The keys were ready for us at the front desk, but there was one thing I totally forgot about until this exact moment. "Shit, I forgot—this bar is cheap as fuck."

Wes smirked. "I can tell that from this dump they stuck us in."

"Well, that's the thing—I couldn't get them to agree to give us more than one hotel room. So we have to share."

Wes shrugged. "Sucks but we'll manage," he said, surprisingly not bitching about it. "Just better be two beds."

"There is, don't worry."

We walked up to the rooms and I, being the nice agent I am, told Wes he could shower first.

"I don't need to shower," Wes replied.

"Really? Even after being on camera in those hot studio lights all day, and then sitting in a car for hours?"

"I'm good."

"Okay, if you say so."

I enjoyed a nice long shower while Wes stretched out on his bed and made a few calls. When I was done he poured us each a drink from my trusty bottle of Jaeger.

"Happy you can drink tonight, Andy?" he asked.

"Obviously it helps, especially if it's a rough gig. But hopefully tonight will be awesome."

Well, it wasn't. Things got off to a bad start when a girl from the bar came to pick us up at the hotel at 10 pm. She was a waitress from the bar, and she'd begged the owner to let her pick Wes up because she was a super fan. Wes was flattered at first, until the nonstop questions started coming.

"So why aren't you and Johanna still together? What happened?. . .Are you dating someone now?. . .What's it like to be on *Real World*?. . . How can I get on the show?. . .Are you still friends with people from your season?. . .Who from the show do you hate the most?. . . How much do you get paid to be on the show?. . .What do you like most in a girl?. . .Wanna drink with me as soon as we get to the bar?"

No, he didn't. He didn't want to have anything to do with her. Wes usually hated answering questions, but he would put on a good show when he had to, especially when getting paid. But here he wasn't even trying to hide his annoyance, responding curtly with one-word answers. This girl didn't seem to pick up on this; she kept rattling on and on, driving us both crazy. She told us her name when she picked us up, but we just wanted to forget everything about her so we forgot her name too.

It's never good when you arrive at a gig with the reality star already in a bad mood. When we got out of the car, Wes pulled me aside. "This nut job is driving me up the wall. I need some weed now!"

"We're about to do an appearance, dude—how about drinks now, and weed later?" I responded.

"Fine but I need a drink ASAP," Wes demanded.

Things didn't get any better when we saw a line of zero people waiting to get in. Nothing. Nobody.

When we walked into the bar the owner came over to greet us. "I haven't had much time to promote," he told us, "so I'm not expecting a big crowd tonight."

Great.

A small crowd meant a small take, so I immediately cut to the chase: "Do you have our $1,200 cash?" Might as well know right away if we were going to get stiffed.

Fortunately he had the money already in an envelope and handed it over to me.

"Thanks. So where do you want Wes?"

"Just wherever—walk around, talk to people," he said. Good to see this guy had a real organized plan.

"Um, okay—can you get us some drinks then?"

He brought us over to the bartender and told her that whatever we wanted was on the house. At least we had free drinks flowing.

But overall the gig sucked, big time. Maybe 40 people max came through the bar doors that night. We made the best of it, and Wes mingled with the few big fans that were there, trying to avoid our annoying driver as much as possible. Which wasn't easy with only around 40 people in the whole place. But it just seemed pointless to be there. It was basically like Wes and I went out to a bar to have a few drinks and happened to run into a few of his fans. None of the wildness I was used to: no crazy contests, no shot-pouring from the bar, no body shots.

And the girls? There was one 919; she was with her boyfriend. The best of the rest were maybe 505 at best, although Wes would say they were 515s. Either way, the Area Code System was not even a factor tonight. I resigned myself to the fact that Wes's mission was not going to be fulfilled.

By the time the endless three-hour gig was up, we couldn't run out of there fast enough. But we really didn't want to deal with the annoying waitress/driver again.

"Listen, we gotta find another way back to the hotel," said Wes. "Plus you promised me weed. We gotta figure that shit out. Now!"

These two girls nearby overheard him and walked over.

"Hey Wes, I'm Beth." Beth, it should be observed, was a 302. "Did I hear you say you needed a ride to the hotel, and that you needed weed?"

"Yes and yes!" Wes responded.

"My friend Kathy and I will drive you guys. And we have weed."

I checked out her friend Kathy. She was a 202. We were going from bad to worse.

"Cool, let's get the fuck out of here then," Wes said.

I rolled my eyes and followed.

The good news was, these girls were way less annoying than our waitress/driver was. They didn't even ask any fangirl questions. Still, I was a little dismayed when Wes invited them to come in with us and have a drink and smoke some weed.

"Whoa. No smoking in the room," I reminded him.

"It'll be fine, trust me, I'll leave the window open."

"Dude, my card is on the room for incidentals and it's a non-smoking room. Last thing I want us some kind of charge on there because they smell weed when we leave."

"They won't smell a thing."

I rolled my eyes again. Wes was playing the big star again. Whatever he said went, and I had to suck it up.

When we got in the room I poured everyone a drink. As I was handing them out, suddenly Beth shouted:

"Shit!"

I was freaked out for a second. "What? Everything okay?"

"Yeah, I just thought I had the weed on me, but I left it at my place," Beth said.

"Ah fuck!" Wes said. "Can you go get it?"

"Only if you come with us for the ride," Beth said coyly.

"That's fine, I'll go. Andy, you in?"

"Nah, fuck this, I'm gonna go to sleep." And I threw in as an aside, "Mission failed, by the way."

"The night isn't over," he said.

"For me it is. Goodnight!"

They left the room to go get the weed. I passed out on my bed, annoyed that the night wasn't even close to what I'd hoped. Oh well, there'd be others…

Two hours later I woke up to the smell of weed, and the sound of giggling in our room. Jesus, they were back! I tried to ignore it and drift back to sleep. I almost succeeded.

But just as I was falling back into dreamland I was jolted awake by a sudden awareness that there were two naked girls in my bed. Wes had told Beth and Kathy to take off their clothes and get under the covers with me while I was sleeping. And they did! They tried to make out with me, and put their hands all over me.

"Girls! I'm sleeping! No thanks," I said.

"But Wes said we should," Kathy said, high and giggling.

Wes was hysterical, laughing his ass off on a chair in the corner of the room.

Yeah, so funny.

"Really, I'm good. I'm just trying to sleep," I said as I tried to push them off the bed.

They reluctantly got off the bed, and I pretended to fall right back to sleep. But I was aggravated and they were all giggling uncontrollably and the room was full of smoke. So I laid there with my eyes closed, listening for a few.

"Wessss," I heard Beth say, "you said if we got under the covers naked with Andy you'd hook up with us after."

Ha! I couldn't believe Wes had told them that. Suckers.

"A promise is a promise, ladies," Wes replied, to my shock. "Let's go."

Wow.

Wes and Andy on the road driving to a gig

They strolled over to his bed, which was next to mine, and the three of them got down to business. The moaning from the girls was loud and resonant, and that combined with their large frames bouncing up and down on the bed made it impossible to sleep. I swore to myself that I'd never share a hotel room with Wes again.

When they were finally finished and things quieted down, I was finally able to drift off. What a night.

When I woke up the next morning the girls were thankfully gone and Wes was still sleeping. I got everything ready and then threw some pillows on him to wake his ass up.

"Let's get out of here, dick," I said to him.

"What are you so pissy about? I was just fulfilling my mission to you."

"Yeah, right."

"Hey, you can't say I failed. I came up with an offer and you declined. Your fault."

"Dude, Beth was a 302, and Kathy was a 202. I wouldn't need any help nailing that shit on my own."

"But you didn't."

"I didn't because I'm not desperate. I guess you are, you seemed to be enjoying yourself," I mocked him.

"I was. Because it was a threesome. And in a threesome, the numbers get added together, and the 0 becomes a 1. So, Beth and Kathy combined were a 514. A reasonably fuckable number."

"Maybe that works for your dick, but not for mine. You can't just add them together. Two losers don't equal one winner."

"It does in a threesome."

"Let's agree to disagree on that one."

"Fine. I still completed my mission. You can't complain that I didn't get you as close to laid as possible."

"You still owe me."

"Get me a shitload of gigs for a shitload of money and then we'll see."

As we drove back to Albany so Wes could catch his flight, I got a call from a Connecticut number.

"May I please speak to Mr. Binder," a rude male voice said when I picked up.

"Yeah, that's me."

"Mr. Binder, this is James from the motel. Our housekeeping service has determined that your room last night was smoked in."

"Smoked in? No!" I said, summoning my shocked outrage.

"The smell is overpowering. We are calling as a courtesy to let you know that we'll be charging your card a $300 cleaning fee."

"Are you serious?!" I yelled into the phone.

"Yes, very. Good day sir," and he hung up.

I glared over at Wes, who was slumped in the passenger seat, totally at peace with the world.

"Thanks a lot, Wes!" I said. "The hotel is charging me $300 because of your fucking smoking!"

"Really?" said Wes. "I wouldn't pay it if I were you. You weren't smoking."

"I have to pay, they're putting it on my card! You said not to worry. You owe me $300!"

"Nah, you're the agent, man. You didn't protest when we smoked."

"I asked you not to."

"You didn't stop us."

"I was sleeping!"

"Excuses, excuses. Oh well, think about all the money I've made you from doing all of our gigs. It all evens out."

"No, I made *you* all the money!"

"However you wanna interpret it. You still wouldn't have gotten the money if I didn't exist. Hey, there's worse things than losing $300," he said philosophically. "Just book me for more events and you'll make that money back in no time."

We drove the next hour in silence. I was totally pissed. I couldn't believe I was putting up with this kind of shit from an untalented overpraised Z-lister like Wes.

But by the time we got back to the airport I was accepting it as a cost of doing business. Wes, as annoying as he could be, had also become a good friend. I was able to act around him in ways that I definitely couldn't with other reality stars. No one else would have agreed to share a room with me, that's for sure.

And ultimately, he was right: the gig was a bust, but so what? There'd be more appearances, more money, and more girls to come. Some of them might even turn out to be 919s! We couldn't win them all, and there would be plenty more for the record books.

CHAPTER 7

CONTEST WINNERS

By 2007 I was on a roll. More and more reality stars were getting in touch and asking me to represent them. I had done extremely right by Wes and Landon and Johanna and Veronica and Rachel, and they were spreading the word about how great I was to work with, telling other reality stars how much money I'd made them, and that they should give me a call to see what kind of magic I could work for them. Not bragging, just stating the facts.

By this time *The Challenge* series had become a huge hit, and MTV had developed a new version for Season 12 with an interesting twist. Before this, *The Challenge* had been stocked with the top cast members from past *Real World* and *Road Rules* seasons; it was a chance to see old favorites in new competition-show type situations. But there was so much demand for the show that MTV couldn't wait for newly-minted popular personalities to emerge from the mother ships. They needed those new faces now, and so began casting complete unknowns to join *The Challenge* right away. This gave birth to *The Fresh Meat Challenge*, where veteran reality stars from *Real World* and *Road Rules* would compete in challenges with an entirely new group of cast members: the "fresh meat."

In *The Fresh Meat Challenge,* two-player teams were made up of a veteran player and a newcomer, one of each sex; the resulting teams squared off in a series of challenges, involving climbing walls, rope ladders, obstacle courses, and so forth. *The Fresh Meat Challenge* turned out to be a big hit, with the winning team of Darrell Taylor and Aviv Melmed walking off with a cool $250,000.

But the real winners were two break-out newcomers, Kenny Santucci and Evan Starkman. Both of these guys became instant fan favorites, and I wasted no time roping them into my stable. At the height of their fame I was getting them both many gigs per month. The girls would go absolutely wild for them. They were young, in shape, good-looking and famous. In fact, these two Z-listers were more recognizable on the street than many A-listers. No wonder their egos got to them. Kenny, in particular, was cocky, self-regarding, and loved the spotlight; he had no qualms about dubbing himself "Mr. Beautiful."

Mario, Andy and Kenny at a hotel before a gig

These guys turned into reality TV superstars. Not only were they invited back to each season of the *Challenge* for many years, but Evan, a Toronto native, got a gig co-hosting specials on MTV Canada and hosting a hit dating show in Canada called *Love Trap*. Kenny, a Jersey native, got a gig hosting MTV specials with the cast of *The Jersey Shore*.

Demand for these two cool dudes was super-high. And because Kenny and Evan had bonded immediately and become best friends, they loved it when I booked them together as a team.

Gigs with the two of them were usually fun as hell. Thousands of the hottest girls would wait hours in line ot see these guys at an appearance. We were tapping into something primal and a little scary in the female psyche. So, of course, I loved booking them together. Their humor and wit balanced off each other well, and the endless eye candy that came to their events was unbelievable.

But the reality was that many small-city bars and clubs just didn't have the budget to book two "stars" at the same time. And unfortunately that was our biggest market. Think about it: someone in New York City or Los Angeles isn't going to give a shit about going out to a nightclub advertising that a "famous" *Real World* cast member will be appearing. These cities have A-listers all over the place; there's little time or desire to seek out a relative nobody. Conversely, it's very common for small towns or cities to embrace the Z-listers. Any brush with fame gets them excited. So I often found myself booking solo club appearances in crappy little towns. Which is how I wound up back in the exciting city of Poughkeepsie, NY, where one of my past customers wanted Kenny for an appearance.

We've already visited Poughkeepsie in this book—that's where I booked Landon Lueck, and where we met those chicks Caitlin Ryder and Nicole "Snooki" Polizzi. So I don't need to go into great detail about it. Located between New York City and Albany, NY, parts of this city can be a depressing and dirty dump. But I love getting paid, and I've never turned down an offer there. For years, the owner of one of Poughkeepsie hottest nightclubs, The Loft, would contact me once a month to bring in a different reality star. Fred is also the owner of The Chance, located downstairs from The

Loft, which is the most famous and legendary music venue in the Hudson Valley.

Fred likes to make business simple and easy. A common Z-lister booking with The Loft included an email exchange like this:

Fred: *hey i need a cast member for saturday, feb. 19, who's available for the cheapest?*

Me: *Hi Fred! Great to hear from you again. We have several cast members available on that date. Kenny or Evan are always great for appearances and live close enough so we wouldn't have to pay for a flight. I can do either one for only $1,500. Let me know. Thanks and look forward to talking to you soon.*

Fred: *yeah kenny is good. lock it in. thx*

And with that, the gig was set. Kenny knew that his appearance at The Loft would include the usual routine of getting on the mic and leading a contest, taking pictures with a lot of girls, and doing many free shots. An easy $1,500 cash, definitely worth the two-hour drive from his hometown in New Jersey.

After the contract was locked in, I didn't really think much about Poughkeepsie until a week before the scheduled event. One day my cellphone vibrated, and as I looked down at the 845 area code number, I immediately thought the worst. "Shit, 845 means it's gotta be Fred from the Loft (he was the only venue I did business with from that area), and he's gotta have some kind of issue if he's calling me just a week before our gig." So I picked up the phone hesitantly.

"Hi, this is Andy," I said, pretending to be enthusiastic.

"Andy. It's Fred." I knew it. Okay, here it comes… "Listen, I want to promote next weekend's Kenny event on our local Top 40 radio station."

That was it? "Cool, no problem, Fred. You can do whatever you want to promote it," I replied, not sure why he was calling to tell me this.

"Well, here's the thing: I want the station to run a contest. People—girls, that is—can call into the station all week long to enter the contest for a date with Kenny. Then on Friday they pick the grand prize winner, and she gets to bring a friend and go on the date with Kenny Saturday night before the Loft appearance." Fred fell silent now, clearly wondering how I would react.

"Okay, so you're saying it will be a nice dinner, completely on you, for me, Kenny, and the two contest winners?" I asked Fred. I made sure I figured myself into the equation.

"Absolutely! Top of the line restaurant, and you guys can order anything you want and drink as much as you want, all on me," Fred responded.

Now this could go real good or real bad, depending, but I decided to take the bait and see what happens. "Okay Fred, let's give it a shot. I'm sure Kenny will be cool with it. But remember, we're doing this for you because we love The Loft," I said, knowing it's always important to make the club owner feel special and do a little ass-kissing so you can keep getting repeat business.

"Oh," I added with a laugh, "can you try to make it so the contest winners are hot?"

"You got it, Andy," Fred laughed back, and hung up.

The rest of the week was a busy one, and it totally slipped my mind to call Kenny and tell him about our date with the contest winner. He called me as usual on the Saturday morning of the appearance.

"Yo, Binder, what time do I need to be in Poughkeepsie tonight?" Kenny asked. We were coming from different directions so we would be meeting there.

"Be at the hotel by 7 pm—cool?"

"7 pm?! Dude, the bars in Poughkeepsie are open all night. I don't even have to be at the club until midnight. Why are you making me get there so early?" Kenny said, annoyed.

"Stop acting like you're some bigwig celebrity," I went back at him, trying to stay calm but getting annoyed myself. "We're getting a free dinner on the club, and I have some girls who are gonna meet up with us for drinks before the event."

"Fine," Kenny said, sounding defeated. "I'll meet you at the hotel at 7."

I hung up, and wondered how Kenny would react when he found out that we were having a "double date" with two contest winners of unknown provenance. Fred promised they would be hot, but who knew? Either way we were getting paid, so who the fuck cared.

As I drove up to the hotel in Poughkeepsie that evening, a huge smile emerged across my face. It was February, but it was over 50 degrees out. Normally it would barely be in the 20s this time of year in New York State. The warmer-than-normal temperatures meant warmer-than-normal girls, dressing slutty and showing lots of skin. This was going to be fun.

I walked into the lobby and was greeted by Cammy, the usual front desk person on duty on Saturdays.

"Welcome back, Andy!" she said to me, a cheerful pep to her voice.

"Thanks, Cammy, it's always good to be in Poughkeepsie," I said with a straight face.

"So, I have both of your rooms on the top floor as usual, both next to each other, king beds, non-smoking," she stated. "The bill goes right to the club so no need to put a credit card down."

Another thing I love about Fred—never an issue with the hotel. He books and pays, and the hotel loves us. These Z-listers are some of the biggest celebrities to come through that town, so why not treat them a little like A-listers? It's all good business.

"Beautiful, thanks again, Cammy." But as I took the keys from her, I noticed a flicker of hesitation on her face. "Something wrong?" I asked.

"Um, well—I hate to ask this, but I'm like really a huge fan of Kenny. He's my favorite on the show and sooo super hot. Do you think I can get a picture with him when he gets here?"

"I will not let him go to his room until he gets a picture with you first," I promised her.

"Thanks Andy, you're awesome!"

"I know," I responded with a smile. "See you in a few."

I went into my hotel room. The king bed was soft, and the room smelled fresh. I got into shower to start getting ready for the night's festivities. The perfect water pressure sent a massaging stream of water on my head and down my back. I wished I could stay in the shower for an hour, but Kenny would be there soon and I wanted to be ready to go. We had a big "date" tonight.

Kenny called to say he was 20 minutes away, so I went down to wait for him in the lobby. A short time later he came barging in the door, singing his personalized greeting chant as always:

"Binder winder, Andy fucking Binder!"

"Kenny Santucci! Welcome to Poughkeepsie!" We hugged. "Before we go upstairs can you take a quick picture with the girl at the front desk? She loves you."

"Yeah of course," Kenny confidently responded.

We walked over to Cammy, who was already googly-eyed over Kenny with a huge grin on her face.

"Look at this beautiful girl," Kenny stated, his cocky attitude already coming to the fore.

"Kenny, it's soooo great to meet you," Cammy said, blushing.

"No baby, it's great to meet *you*," Kenny responded. "Come in my arms, let's take a picture."

Cammy handed me the camera, as usual. It's my unwritten responsibility; when going anywhere with a Z-lister, I'm the official Picture Taker to the Stars. No one ever asks; it's assumed.

But I happily comply. I get a kick out of it.

I snapped the picture of the two of them. "That's gonna be my new Facebook profile pic," Cammy said enthusiastically.

"It better be," Kenny said.

We headed off to the elevator to get Kenny settled. A grateful Cammy called after him, "I love you, Kenny!"

"Love you too, babe," Kenny responded.

We hopped on the elevator. "So, good to see you, Binder. What's the plan?" Kenny asked me.

Ah, the fateful moment had arrived. "The plan is, you get ready, and then we're walking a few blocks to a restaurant to meet some contest winners," I said with a practiced casualness.

"Contest winners?" Kenny shot back. "What the fuck are you talking about?"

"Yeah, sorry, I forgot to mention it sooner. The club owner set up this contest with a local radio station, and the winner gets a date with you, so we're meeting the winner and her friend at a restaurant and getting a good free meal out of it." With that the elevator door opened and I quickly stepped off and walked down the hall towards our rooms.

Kenny followed silently. I tried to stay cool as I anxiously awaited his response. Kenny is hit-or-miss. Sometimes he would complain about the tiniest things and act like a high-ego A-lister. Other times, he goes with the flow and is happy to do whatever I ask. I waited to see which way the wave would break this time.

"Well," Kenny finally said, "these contest winners better be fucking hot."

I laughed. "That's what I told the owner. We'll see."

I went into his hotel room with him to make sure he didn't take his time or get distracted. Not every reality star understands the importance of staying on schedule. Some love to take their sweet-ass time getting ready, showering, brushing their hair, and making themselves smell good. Kenny Santucci wasn't the worst offender, but the self-proclaimed "Mr. Beautiful" could learn to cut some minutes off his gig prep time.

"Hurry up, man," I said. "We gotta be at the restaurant in 15 minutes."

"Relax, I'm gelling my hair. I'll be done in a few," he replied.

Finally, after asking me four times about which shirt he looked best in, the "talent" was ready to go. We headed outside and walked towards the restaurant. The streets were deserted, and I noted all the out-of-business store fronts in the sad and depressing city. Such a shame.

But I just took a deep breath of that surprisingly warm Poughkeepsie air, and told myself to not let Kenny piss me off tonight. We needed to have a great time, and if we didn't drink too much we would. Most people would jump at the chance of getting a free 5-star dinner, then having VIP and open bar all night at a nightclub. We were getting paid for it. Life was good.

We found the restaurant easily, since it was one of the few places open, and went inside. Before I was able to say a word to the hostess, she recognized Kenny and immediately escorted us to a private table in the back.

"Thanks so much for coming, gentleman," she said. "Your dates will be here shortly. In the meantime, can I get you some drinks?"

"I'll take a gin and tonic," I said.

"Same for me," Kenny added.

I checked out the scene at the restaurant. Happy couples

dating. Married couples on their first night out in a while. Groups of friends. The scene was festive, and the warm glow of the table lamps worked to mellow my anxiety of the "date" that was about to happen.

Then Kenny weighed in.

"So Binder, have you talked to these contest winners yet?"

"No, I haven't."

"What are their names?"

"I don't know."

"You don't know?"

"Kenny, I was just told where we have to go and what time we had to be here," I responded.

"So you're telling me that you have no idea if these girls are hot, or if they're pigs?" Kenny said.

"No idea."

"Dammit, Binder, why do you get me into these situations?" Good question. Why did I get *myself* into these situations? "Look, if these girls walk in and they're huge fat pigs, then we're just going to walk out without even talking to them—okay?" Kenny asked.

"Um, well, we have an obligation to at least be here for a few," I responded.

"Maybe *you* have an obligation. I don't."

"We'll keep it quick if they're that disgusting, so relax."

"I have a bad feeling about this, Binder," Kenny said.

We got our gin-and-tonics and guzzled them down fast. We both wanted to be ready to face whatever was going to come through that door. Hey, it was already twenty minutes past the time we were supposed to meet these girls. Maybe they weren't going to show and we'd be off the hook anyway.

All of a sudden I looked toward the door and saw two gorgeous girls walk in. When I say gorgeous, I mean hot as hell. 11 out of 10s. On the Area Code rating system, 919s. Top of the top.

And they were wearing tiny skirts, with tops that only covered their breasts. Their entire stomachs were exposed, including their sexy belly button rings. One tall and tan with long dark hair. The other shorter, with large breasts, dirty blonde hair, and blue eyes.

Kenny and I glanced at each other and grinned. This would most definitely not be a speed-date.

"Hi girls," I said as I stood up to introduce myself. "I'm Andy, Kenny's agent. You must be the contest winners?"

"Yeah, I'm Stacey," said the tall brunette, "and this is Brooke."

"Cool, great to meet you both. And this is Kenny," I said.

"A pleasure, ladies," Kenny said in his sexiest voice. The girls giggled and sat down. So far, so very good.

At first, the conversation was slow. The girls were clearly nervous, eating with a famous Z-lister and all. Kenny and I did our best to break the ice and get the ball rolling.

"So, tell us about yourselves," I said.

"Well, we go to Marist, it's a college in Poughkeepsie," Brooke replied.

"Yeah, I know it. Division 1 basketball," Kenny said.

"It's a fun school. We party a lot," Stacey said.

"Exactly what we plan on doing tonight," I added.

"Us too," both girls said in unison.

Oh boy.

Our meals came and they were fantastic. My steak was cooked to perfection, and Kenny was pleased with his pasta. The girls both ordered salads. As we were finishing dinner Kenny gave me the universal look—"invite these girls to hang out with us." That's part of my job. Many of these reality stars don't want to be seen as the ones pursuing. They'd rather be pursued. So if they want someone, and they aren't getting pursued yet, they designate a friend to take the risk for them. Fulfilling my role as agent, tour manager, and friend, I knew what Kenny wanted right away. And, if I was reading these girls correctly, there wouldn't be any rejection.

"So ladies," I said, "Kenny and I are heading back to the hotel for a drink before we hit the club. You wanna come pre-game with us?"

"Yes!" Stacey said, no hesitation.

"Definitely!" Brooke agreed.

Kenny looked at me, smiled and nodded. I had done good. We thanked the waitress, left a tip, and headed out of the restaurant with the two girls. The whole walk back to the hotel featured the girls giggling and Kenny flirting. It was getting interesting.

As we walked into the hotel, Cammy looked over at us and smiled. I gave her a wave, and we headed over to the elevator. We got out at the top floor and I told the crew that we could all have drinks in my room (most of the time the reality stars don't want visitors in their rooms. Only the select few "lucky" ones get to enter the Z-list star's inner sanctum. So usually my room was where we ended up pre-gaming before a nightclub appearance).

I put the key card into the door and it flashed green and clicked open. I was the first one in, followed by Kenny, Brooke and Stacey. The door slammed shut behind them.

And that's when it started. Less than five seconds later, Stacey started removing her clothes. All of them. Without any coaxing. She just started taking them all off! Kenny and I started laughing. We didn't ask her to strip down, but who were we to stop her?

"Come here, Kenny," the spectacularly naked Stacey said seductively.

Kenny didn't move right away. "What for?" he jokingly responded.

"For this," Stacey said, and she ran across the room and leaped on top of him like a horny gazelle. Kenny was so startled he didn't know what to do. But he didn't have to do anything, Stacey was providing all the forward motion. Kenny's Z-list fame was getting him practically raped in my hotel room with an audience. But he wasn't complaining.

"Wait, what about Brooke? Is she gonna get naked for Andy?" Kenny asked, trying to be a good friend.

Brooke started to take off her clothes, but she clearly didn't want to hook up with me, I could see that. Hey, you win some, you lose some, and I was just getting a kick out of this whole hotel room experience. Plus, we didn't even get to the club yet; hopefully I'd find a girl there.

"It's all good," I said, "let's just have some drinks."

"Sure," Stacey responded, as she slipped her hands down Kenny's pants while putting her breasts in his face. "But me and Kenny are gonna go in the shower first."

"We are?" Kenny asked, clearly enjoying himself.

Stacey grabbed Kenny's arm and escorted him to the bathroom. They didn't even bother closing the door. The sounds inside indicated a great time being had by all.

I looked over at Brooke, who was now completely naked herself. "We might as well do a shot," I said.

We both gulped down a shot of some cheap-ass vodka. Damn, it tasted disgusting. But after the shot, Brooke got a scheming look in her eye.

"Let's go downstairs," she said.

"Now?" I asked.

"Yeah, now—let's go!" She grabbed my hand, opened the door, and led me out of the room into the hall. She was still naked.

"What are we doing?!" I asked, as we walked over to the elevator.

"Having fun," she giggled. These Poughkeepsie girls sure knew how to enjoy themselves.

So we took the elevator down. I had no idea what was going to be waiting for us in the first-floor lobby. As it turned out, when the doors opened, the lobby was pretty empty. Brooke was a little disappointed—here she was, naked and unafraid, and nobody to see her—but then we heard music playing at the end of the hall. We saw the sign with the arrow pointing back to the Banquet Room.

"It must be a wedding!" Brooke exclaimed with delight. And she started running down the hall, her bare ass bouncing away from me.

"Wait—It might be a bar mitzvah!" I jokingly yelled, as I chased after her.

But it was a wedding. And Brooke didn't waste any time crashing it. She raced right out to the dance floor, raising her arms triumphantly—ta-da!

Needless to say, the reactions of the wedding guests were priceless. "What the hell is that girl doing in here?" I heard the maid of honor scream.

"Damn, this wedding is way better than I expected!" a groomsman proclaimed.

"You're ruining my daughter's wedding!" the father of the bride shouted.

But the band members were enjoying it, and they kept playing as Brooke commandeered the dance floor and showed off her moves. It only took a few minutes before Security arrived, and they escorted my naked friend Brooke off the dance floor. Brooke waved goodbye to her many new fans, and we left the Banquet Room to a mixture of cheers and shocked grumbling.

We were brought to a back room, and Brooke was given a towel to put over her. Which she declined; she was very comfortable with her nakedness. Undaunted, I summoned my agent skills to try to sweet-talk Security.

"I'm so sorry about this, sir. We're just really excited to be in Poughkeepsie, and things got a little out of hand. You see, we're on tour with a reality star from MTV and we're appearing at The Loft tonight… Again, I'm very sorry and please let me know if there's anything we can do to make up for our immature actions…."

The security officer's eyebrows rose. "Oh, you're with MTV! I heard you guys were in town. I watch those shows all the time. Me and my girlfriend are huge fans," he said.

"I'm happy to hear that, sir," I responded.

"Yeah, she's gonna get a kick out of this, when I tell her how I pulled a naked girl from MTV out of a wedding," the security officer said.

Well, she wasn't from MTV. But I didn't need to clarify this with the security guy.

"This'll make her night!" He then assumed his more professional security voice. "Look, you guys just go back to your room, and no more nude gallivanting through the hotel. Deal?"

"You got it sir. Thanks again for your help—you and your staff do an amazing job here," I replied, making sure to kiss just a little more ass as Brooke and I walked out of the back room and headed upstairs to my hotel room.

We laughed the whole way back up to the room. By the time we got there, Kenny and Stacey were getting out of the shower.

"You guys have fun?" I asked.

"You know it, bro," Kenny responded.

"How about you guys?" Stacey asked as she dried herself with a towel. "What were you doing?"

"Naked wedding crashing," Brooke said proudly. Stacey and Brooke high-fived. "But thanks to Andy I wasn't arrested."

"Binder winder, the miracle worker!" Kenny said. "Always working the reality TV angle whenever there's a problem."

"Yeah dude, I take advantage of your Z-list stardom wherever I can," I said.

The girls started cracking up.

"Fuck you, I'm no Z-list star. A-list all the way," Kenny said, while not doing a good job keeping a straight face.

"Whatever makes you sleep better at night," I responded.

Laughing, we all had a few more drinks while the girls got dressed. Hard to believe, the gig hadn't even started yet, and we'd already partied with two naked women. I had to hand it to Fred, the date with the contest winners was definitely a success.

It was 11:30 now and time to get over to the nightclub, which was only a block from the hotel. As we walked down the block we saw a line of about 300 people waiting to get into the club. Kenny and I looked at each other. Not bad for Poughkeepsie!

The bouncer recognized us and escorted us upstairs to the VIP area. Fred handed Kenny the mic and had him say hi to the crowd. Five more girls came over to join us in VIP, and our personal cocktail waitress brought us all shots and beers. Yes, tonight was definitely a good night.

CHAPTER 8

BEADS AND BOBOS

MARDI GRAS, BABY!

In the midst of juggling reality star appearances and building up my client list, I got an invite to New Orleans from my brother who was attending Law School at Tulane University. It was his second year there, and, knowing me and my lifestyle, he knew I'd just love the Mardi Gras experience. Could I possibly tear myself away from my job long enough to come down for a visit?

Are you kidding? A free place to stay in New Orleans during prime Mardi Gras time? How could I turn that down?

I went down and met him and his fiancée (whom he married a year later) at their place in the Garden District. My brother assured me that the New Orleans Garden District was a prime location to view all of the Mardi Gras parades. A nice area with historic houses, it was located just a few minutes from Bourbon Street (and don't think I didn't get to enjoy Bourbon Street!).

This was my first time in Nola, so I had to experience it all—the jazz, the crawfish, po-boys, beignets at Café Du Monde, a muffaletta from Central Market, gumbo and jambalaya. And the Bourbon Street culture of Hurricane drinks that you could bring from bar to bar, drinking from open containers on the street, and giving out beads for being flashed. All times of year on Bourbon you'll find girls baring their breasts for a 10-cent bead. It's the culture.

I was expecting great food, great music, great drinks and some great females on display. But I wasn't prepared for the absolute insanity of the parades. That was a part of the Mardi Gras experience I didn't really understand before I witnessed it first-hand.

The parades are run by organizations called Krewes. If you're a member of a Krewe, you get to ride in the Mardi Gras parades on floats, and throw out beads to the crowds. There's a membership fee to join a Krewe, and the larger the Krewe and the more elaborate the parade, the more expensive the membership fee is. Fees can run to several thousand dollars a year.

The biggest Krewe parades run on the Saturday, Sunday and Monday leading up to Fat Tuesday itself. This was the very weekend I picked to be there with my brother. The parades lasted for hours and hours, and hundreds of thousands of people lined the streets screaming for "throws." A Throw is the term used for everything the Krewe members toss out from the floats. Yes, it's mostly beads, but it could also be anything from stuffed animals to fruits. The parades meander through the city, and the closer they get to downtown and the Canal/Bourbon Street area, the wilder things get. Families will wisely view the parades uptown, and leave downtown to the drunken mobs.

Even cooler, each of the Super Krewe parades has celebrity monarchs, as well as famous musicians who perform at the ball at the end of the parade. Tickets for the ball are usually well over $100, and attended by thousands.

Okay, so I was having a great time just soaking all this sublime craziness in, but that didn't mean my business instincts had gone into sleep mode. When I saw that these parades featured celebrities on the floats, the wheels started turning. How perfect this would be for my reality stars! Maybe my guys weren't as famous as some of the big shots I was seeing now, but hey, why not? Plus it looked like the stars themselves were having a blast, and I wanted to be a part of that. Watching the parades was itself a great experience, but imagine being up there with a celebrity! And since so far I was accomplishing everything I tried to do, my head was big enough to think I could make it happen.

When I got back home the next week, I went right to work researching the Super Krewes online; I called the numbers and sent e-mails to every contact I found.

No one answered and no one called back. I was bummed.

But then surprisingly I did get one response e-mail, from one of the Super Krewes- The Krewe of Orpheus. I was informed that my information was being forwarding to Jack, the staff member who coordinated the celebrity monarchs for the Krewe of Orpheus parade, and that he would be giving me a call sometime that week.

I was ecstatic! The Krewe of Orpheus was originally founded in 1993 by legendary singer Harry Connick Jr.! Their parade always took place on Lundi Gras, the Monday night before Fat Tuesday. If there was one Krewe I wanted to be a part of, this was it!

I tried not to get my hopes up, but that was impossible. All I could think about was getting paid to ride on a float in one of New Orleans' biggest and best Mardi Gras parades.

Two days later I got the call.

"Can I speak to Andy, please," said a heavily southern-accented voice.

"This is Andy."

"Hi Andy, this is Jack with the Krewe of Orpheus in New Orleans? I got a message that you'd like to bring some reality stars down to our parade next year as guests?"

"Yes!" I responded with enthusiasm, "I work with a bunch of reality stars from MTV, and some of them would love to come down for the parade," even though I wasn't totally sure which ones yet.

"Well, here's how it works. We provide your hotel rooms, and an invite to our VIP Krewe party on the Sunday night before the parade. And of course a spot on a prime float in our parade. How does that sound?" It sounded beautiful!

"But that's all," Jack added. "You'll have to pay your own way to New Orleans."

"There's no talent appearance fee?" I asked, somewhat deflated.

"That's not how we work. We consider it an honor to be featured in our parades, so we don't typically pay any talent fee."

Well, that presented something of an obstacle. The only thing my clients considered an honor came in the form of cash, and I tended to feel the same way. Still, I wanted to ride that float!

"Okay, thanks for the info, Jack. Can I get back to you in a week or so?"

"Yeah, no rush, we're still a year out."

I hung up and thought about who to ask. Wes wasn't going to do it for free, I knew that. And Landon's fees were so high at the moment that I doubted he'd be interested either.

But *Real World: Sydney* had just started airing, and I thought some newbies might be down for the experience. I asked Wes for some numbers (it's a small world, the reality world, and they all seem to know each other), and made a few calls to introduce myself and see if there was any interest. My first call was to *Real World: Sydney* star Dunbar Merrill.

"Hey Andy," said Dunbar, "I've heard your name before from some of last season's cast members, they suggested I should contact you at some point."

Very cool. I was finally becoming a household name in the reality star club.

I plunged in. "So, I know you're looking for paid gigs, but I have this really cool opportunity that you might be down for. I have a connection with the Krewe of Orpheus, they do a big Mardi Gras parade in New Orleans, and they're looking to bring in some reality stars to be their celebrity guest monarchs next year. They pay for the hotels but not for the flights, and there's no talent fee, but. . ."

"Stop right there," Dunbar interrupted.

Shit. He didn't even let me get past the "but." I guess I was kidding myself to think these guys cared about anything other than money...

"Did you say the Krewe of Orpheus, during Mardi Gras?" Dunbar asked. "I love Mardi Gras! And that's one of the biggest parades! I grew up in Mississippi and would always go party in New Orleans for Mardi Gras, especially when I was in college. I never expected I'd get a chance to be in one of the parades. This is awesome! I'm totally in!"

Well, that was an unexpected twist.

"That's great!" I said. "Do you think anyone else from *Sydney* would be interested?"

"Sure, I bet Isaac and Cohutta would be down." Isaac and Cohutta were his male co-stars from *Real World Sydney*. "Give me a day to talk to them, I'll get them on board. I'll call you tomorrow."

I didn't even have to wait until tomorrow. Dunbar called me back that evening to tell me Isaac and Cohutta were in, too. Which was perfect: the three guys starring in the current *Real World* season. By this time next year there'd be a new season airing, and these guys would likely be demanding high fees, but I had nabbed them for nothing. And I was going to get to experience Mardi Gras in New Orleans, the way celebrities do. I couldn't wait for next February to roll around.

Business, clients and gigs kept me busy during the year, and the money kept rolling in. But I cared most about that unpaid Mardi Gras event coming up. I met Isaac, Cohutta and Dunbar in person at gigs several times during the year, and they kept the hype going too. Everyone seemed so excited about it.

And when my buddy Mario found out I was riding a Mardi Gras float in New Orleans, he begged me to let him in on the action.

"Dude, I love Mardi Gras. Bobos everywhere! Come on, let me get on the float with you guys."

I wasn't sure if I could swing getting Mario placed on the float itself—he was no celebrity—but then I remembered Wes' reaction when he met Mario. "Hey, you know, New Orleans can get pretty rowdy, especially during Mardi Gras. Maybe we can tell everyone you're our security guy who's on tour with us?" That might work out perfectly; Mario's huge frame would fend off all the crazies.

"Sure, as long as I can be a security guy that drinks, does body shots, and sees bobos, then I'm all in."

But there was one thing I had to make clear: "You're gonna have to pay for your own flight, *and* your own hotel room." There was no way in hell I was sharing my room with Mario the snoring bear again.

"Yeah, no problem, I just wanna experience the parade."

And I just wanted to experience a good night's sleep.

February finally came. We were all coming from different directions to New Orleans, but we managed to show up at the airport around the same time. We shared a shuttle into the city, and normally what would have been a twenty-minute ride took over an hour. It was Mardi Gras—tourists and parades blocked the streets everywhere. The closest the shuttle could get to the hotel was four blocks away, so we hopped out, grabbed our bags, and trekked through the packed streets to the Sheraton on Canal Street.

But no problem—it was great to be back in New Orleans, and this year had a much different vibe. Instead of staying at my brother's place, I was at the Sheraton on world-famous Canal Street, a block from Bourbon, with three famous reality stars and my good friend/security guard in tow. It was 65 degrees and sunny, and coming from a wintry upstate New York, it felt amazing.

After getting settled, we grabbed a drink at the hotel bar then headed right outside. You can bring your drinks anywhere outside in New Orleans, open containers are good to go. Amazing shit. So we walked over to Bourbon Street, drinks in hand. The street was packed with partiers, and girls looking for beads. Luckily Mario came prepared, with what would become known as his legendary Duck Beads. He had ordered them online: they were yellow-bead necklaces with four squeaky rubber ducks attached. Most people on Bourbon had just the regular cheapo beads, so Mario's were an instant hit. The girls flocked to him, flashing him for a duck bead.

"Remind you of Smitty's Law?" he asked me.

"Only better," I responded.

Dunbar, Isaac and Cohutta were getting a kick out of it. Mario had 24 duck beads around his neck, and he ran out of them in about twenty minutes. "That's forty-eight bobos in less than half-an-hour," he grinned proudly, and I was impressed with his math skills.

"Yeah, but now what are you gonna do? You're all out."

"Don't worry," he assured us. "I ordered 30 boxes, they were delivered right to the hotel. Plenty more for later."

Can't say Mario didn't have his priorities straight. He hadn't paid his mortgage on his condo for years, and was holding out until he could negotiate a better deal or the bank kicked him out. But spending close to $1,000 on duck beads for Mardi Gras was a sound investment. He had told me many times, he'd rather deal with a terrible credit score and get to experience life and travel and alcohol and bobos, than waste money on a mortgage.

The afternoon was going great, until I got a text from Jack with the Krewe of Orpheus. I saw his name pop up and got nervous. What's wrong?

Jack: *You guys make it into the city and get your rooms at the hotel?*

Cool, he was just checking in on us making sure we're all good.

Me (looking down at my phone as the others were walking ahead in the crowd): *Yeah, thanks again, we're -*

At that moment, in the middle of my text, my phone was snatched from my hand. Some teenage kid on Bourbon Street had grabbed it and started running. I was in shock for a moment, and looked around for help, but the rest of my crew was way ahead and didn't see what was happening.

So I turned and ran after this idiot punk alone. The adrenaline rush was taking over as I thought about not having my phone while in New Orleans. A disaster! I pushed everyone out of my way, hoping to find a cop during my chase, but not seeing one. I caught up to the kid a minute later and grabbed his arm.

"What the FUCK do you think you're doing?!" I yelled at him as the adrenaline continued to pour through me.

The idiot dropped the phone on the street.

"What are you talking about?" he said, innocently, with his hands up.

I picked up the phone. "*This* is what I'm talking about! You think you can just steal a phone out of someone's hands? Hell no! Let's go find a cop, I'm getting your ass arrested!"

He yanked his arm free away and started running in the other direction. I chased after him again, even though I had my phone back, determined to see justice done. Unfortunately, he ran up to a group of about fifteen huge guys, probably in their mid-20s, who seemed to be part of his "crew."

One of the hulking characters took a step towards me. "Is there a problem here?" he asked, with a hint of menace. For all I knew, he had a gun on him.

"This kid tried to steal my phone, that's the problem," I said.

The huge guy looked at the kid. "Doesn't look like he has a phone to me. So I'll ask again, is there a problem here?" The entire crew moved closer to me in the process.

It was around that time that I suddenly lost my thirst for justice. "Fuck it, not worth my time," I said, wisely recognizing that the risk of any violence here would not end well for me. I hurried away quickly through the crowded street, trying to catch up to Dunbar, Isaac, Cohutta and Mario far ahead. I saw a sign for a to-go beer stand, and figured they would be there. They were.

"Where'd you go?" Isaac asked me.

"Some kid tried to steal my phone. I got it back, but I almost got killed in the process," I responded dramatically, while still catching my breath.

"Yeah man, gotta be careful on the streets of New Orleans," Dunbar said.

Noted.

And with that we went on our way to get more drinks and see more breasts. Around 6 pm it was time to head back to the Sheraton to get ready for the Krewe of Orpheus VIP party. This party is held the night before the Krewe of Orpheus parade at a luxury hotel with a huge balcony, on the famous corner of Canal and Bourbon, with prime viewing for the major Sunday night parade. I knew free drinks would be flowing all night, so I definitely wanted to pace myself.

Jack called me twenty minutes before the party was scheduled to start at 7. "Never heard back from you, are you in the city?" he asked.

"Oh shit yeah, sorry man. My phone almost got stolen and I totally forgot to text you back."

"Well, I'm glad it wasn't stolen, and I'm glad you guys are here.

I'll meet you out in front of the party in twenty minutes and walk you guys up."

The streets were all blocked off for the parade, and the crowds on the sidewalks were insane. It took us a half hour to just walk a block. I forgot we were on Mardi Gras time. But we made it, and Jack met us downstairs. He was a short guy, in his late 40s, very energetic and enthusiastic. I introduced him to the reality stars and our "security" Mario, and he brought us upstairs.

"So there are two areas," Jack explained as we got to the top of the stairs. "This area on the left is for the Orpheus VIPs who pay hundreds of dollars to be at this party. The area through the doors on the right is the celebrity VIP room, and VIP balcony. It's for our celebrity guests for the parade, their guests, and the leaders of Orpheus. It's open bar and all the food you want. Here's your celebrity wristbands for access. Have fun!"

We turned the corner into the room and found an amazing array of top-shelf drinks and a decadent food selection. When we stepped outside on the balcony we found ourselves overlooking the corner of Canal Street and Bourbon Street. There were thousands of parade-viewers piled together below, while we were very comfortable one story above. It was surreal.

Ever the businessman, I kept an eye out for any real (i.e. non Z-list) celebrities I could schmooze. There were a lot of actors from TV shows that everyone else seemed to watch but I didn't, so I wasn't really interested in talking to them. But then, on the right side of the balcony looking out onto the street, I spotted a very familiar face that brought back memories of my high school and college days. It was Lance Bass from N'Sync!

"Mr. Bass," I said as I walked over to his side. "I'm Andy and I'm a big fan. I also book celebrities for appearances, and I'd love to work with you sometime." I handed him my business card.

Lance shook my hand and took the card. "Yeah thanks, I'll forward this to my manager," he said politely, but he was clearly not interested in talking further, business or otherwise.

Not one to give up on the first try, I was ready to spring another slick line on the Bass and see if I could reel him in, when suddenly Isaac and Cohutta came barging over. "Lance! Lance!" Isaac shouted.

What the fuck, I was thinking to myself. I hope these guys don't do something embarrassing.

"Lance!" Isaac repeated, in case Lance was going deaf. "Sing an N'Sync song with us! Mario! Come over and film this shit with your phone!"

"Hey, Isaac, relax," I said. "Don't bug Mr. Bass, he's just chilling, waiting for the parade. Give him some space."

Lance seemed to appreciate my respectful attitude. Isaac didn't.

"No, it's cool!" Isaac responded. "Come on Lance, let's do some N'Sync right now!"

Lance stood there, smiling tightly, clearly hoping this annoying pain in the ass would go away.

But Isaac persisted. He started singing. "*I lie awake, I drive myself crazy, drive myself crazy, thinking of you.*"

Cohutta joined in. "*Made a mistake when I let you go baby.*"

"Ha ha," Lance laughed uncomfortably. "Not sure if I even remember all the words to that one."

"Yeah you do, come on, roll with it!" Isaac enthusiastically shouted.

Lance VERY reluctantly joined in on the last line of the chorus. "*I drive myself crazy, wanting you the way that I do, wanting you the way that I do. . .*"

"Yes! Amazing! Awesome! Private N'Sync concert! You're the best, Lance!" Isaac yelled.

"Good to meet you guys," Lance said, and walked away from us.

As soon as Lance was out of hearing range. I turned on Isaac. "Dude! What the fuck! You gotta be polite when you see real celebrities. We're lucky to be here. Don't ruin it for us."

"Relax, Andy," Isaac said. "We're celebrities too, we can have fun and do what we want."

"No we *can't!* Orpheus is a very exclusive organization. If you piss them off, or get the celebrities mad at you, we won't get invited back. Simple as that." I was really annoyed with him, and I let him know it, client or not.

"Okay, whatever, I'm getting a drink." He and Cohutta walked over to the bar.

Word must have gotten back to Jack about Isaac's antics, because he had his eye on us the rest of the night, making sure everyone behaved. And for the most part we did. Except for the climax of the night, so to speak.

The highlight of the annual Orpheus VIP party is when the major Sunday night parade, the Krewe of Bacchus, stops right in front of the Orpheus party balcony, and the celebrity monarch stands up on the float and toasts the celebrity monarchs of Orpheus. It's an annual tradition. The celebrities of both parades get on mics and salute each other, while the thousands of people on parade route on Canal Street hear and witness the toast.

That year, in 2008, the Krewe of Bacchus celebrity monarch was Hulk Hogan. When the Bacchus float stopped right in front of our balcony, the Hulkster himself stood up and took out the mic.

"Brother! The Krewe of Bacchus salutes the Krewe of Orpheus!" Hulk Hogan confidently shouted into the mic in his hoarse booming voice.

"The Krewe of Orpheus salutes the Krewe of Bacchus!" Lance Bass and the actors who I didn't know shouted back to him.

And everyone took a drink. It was a pretty cool moment.

And then Isaac grabbed the mic.

"Hulk! Show us your nipples!" Isaac yelled into the mic. "Here's mine," he said as he lifted up his shirt.

An Orpheus official grabbed the mic away from Isaac, and Hulk Hogan just smiled and sat back down on the float, which went on its way as the parade moved forward.

Jack was furious. "That was completely unacceptable!" he yelled at Isaac. "There are families down there on the streets, and we don't run things like that here. Any more behavior like that and we'll be forced to ask you all to leave and not ride in the parade tomorrow."

"Okay, okay," Isaac said, not really seeming to care.

"We got it, Jack," I quickly added. "I'll take care of it."

I pulled Isaac aside, pissed off as hell.

"Listen, man, don't you get it? You're lucky to be here! You're not at the celebrity level of these people, and you can't just act any way you want. The real celebrities are acting appropriately. You need to, too."

"Okay, chill out Andy, I'm getting another drink," he responded.

And off he went, oblivious. He was that most dreaded of animals, the reality star who had lost touch with reality. Bamboozled by their own publicity, these totally ordinary guys and girls start to think they really are God's gift, and they self-inflate into clueless, ego-inflated jerks. Isaac, alas, was a prime example. And we were stuck with him.

Mario thought the whole thing was funny, but he wouldn't be laughing so hard if Isaac got us kicked off the Orpheus float. Fortunately the rest of the night went uneventfully, mostly because Isaac left early to go party on Bourbon Street.

And the next day dawned beautifully. The weather was perfect and the excitement was in the air. It was a great day for a parade, and we'd be riding in a celebrity float in the Krewe of Orpheus, throwing out beads to thousands of people. It would be a legendary experience. And at the New Orleans Convention Center where the parade kicked off, everyone was showing up on time, ready to go, even though we were all hung over.

Yes, everything was going great. Until I saw Isaac.

Slowly walking down the convention center hallway were my three reality stars: Dunbar, Isaac and Cohutta. Dunbar and Cohutta looked fine, but Dunbar had a dark, unsettled look on his face. And immediately I could see why.

Isaac was wearing a pink thong. Nothing else. Just a pink thong.

"Isaac, what the fuck!" I yelled at him. "They're not going to allow that kind of outfit on the float!"

"It's Mardi Gras, it's fine," he assured me.

"No it's not!"

Before I had the chance to hustle him out of sight, Jack spotted him and ran over.

"Isaac, no! No!" he said, as if yelling at a dog. "Not acceptable! You need to be wearing clothes!"

"These *are* clothes," Isaac said jokingly.

Jack was not amused. "This is the only time we're telling you this. If you don't get some clothes on right away, you'll be asked to leave immediately. All of you!"

That was all we had to hear. The four of us—Mario, Dunbar, Cohutta and me—we all started bitching at Isaac to get dressed now. We weren't going to miss this parade because of him and his stupid pink thong. He was overmatched, so he reluctantly gave in, but he was annoyed about it.

Well, that was it for me: I made a mental note that I'd never bring Isaac to Mardi Gras again, if Orpheus even allowed us back. But I didn't tell him that. I wanted him on his best behavior for the rest of the trip.

And at least there were no more issues that day. And it was absolutely a surreal experience. Being on the float, tossing beads and other random items to thousands of screaming parade-goers, ending up at a huge ball with thousands of people inside...No words could do it justice. You had to be there.

But I'll try to do it a little more justice with the following year's experience. Because that was even better. And yes, we were invited back.

ABOUT A MONTH AFTER WE GOT back from the 2008 Mardi Gras I called Jack. I wanted to give a little time to let any hard feelings dissipate.

"Jack, it was so awesome meeting you and everyone at Orpheus last month. You guys were amazing, and we had a great experience. Thank you again!"

"Thanks Andy, it was great meeting you too. Everyone loved you guys. Except for Isaac."

I figured there was no way of avoiding that subject. "Yeah, I know, sorry about him. I had no idea he'd act that way. I would never invite him back. Assuming you invite *us* back..."

"We actually did talk it over, and we'd be happy to have you and your reality stars back next year. As long as you don't bring Isaac."

"Awesome, thanks so much, Jack! We really appreciate it, and we won't let you down! Let's talk when it gets closer."

As Mardi Gras 2009 drew near, I finalized everything with Jack. Mario was coming again to provide Security (of course) with his endless supply of duck beads. He had been very professional with the Orpheus people, since he understood Mardi Gras and the importance and the honor of being a part of the parade. I also decided to bring Kenny Santucci and Evan Starkman this time around. They were still huge on the reality circuit and I figured they'd be big hits at the parade; the ladies would love them. They were both excited about the chance to experience it, even though they weren't going to get paid. They recognized the honor of going.

When the time came to head down to New Orleans, the excitement and anticipation was high. We were hoping to get the same VIP treatment as last year, this time without the hassles of Isaac's disrespect. At the last minute my friend Justin (Snooki's human seatbelt), asked if he could join us. We had the space so I figured why not. I knew he'd really appreciate the experience as well.

Kenny, Evan, and Dunbar at a Krewe of Orpheus
VIP party during Mardi Gras

So the six of us met down in New Orleans and formed quite the crew: Mario, Justin, Dunbar, Kenny, Evan and me. We made up "reality star Mardi Gras VIP passes" to wear around town and showcase who we were. I explained the deal to everyone, and Dunbar reiterated my point of being respectful. This was our chance to show Orpheus that most of us in the reality world are great people to work with.

I figured we might not get as many perks as last year. And we didn't. We got more.

Jack told me to have everyone meet in the hotel lobby at 6:30pm for the annual Sunday night Orpheus VIP party. Another group of celebrities were also waiting there for Jack: the cast of *Reno 911*, all in character! It was hilarious. Then Jim Belushi came off the elevator into the lobby. The celebrities were everywhere!

Jack arrived and escorted Jim Belushi into a limo. Then he ushered our crew and the cast of *Reno 911* into a big limo bus that was directly behind the limo. New Orleans police cars and motorcycles got in front of Jim Belushi's limo and behind our limo bus, and we took off. Holy shit, we were in a celebrity motorcade in New Orleans for Mardi Gras!

Police cleared the crowds away as we drove through the closed-off streets to get to the VIP party on the corner of Canal and Bourbon. The red carpet was out and the crowd was roped off as we were all whisked from the limos, down the carpet and up the stairs to the party, with parade watchers screaming for autographs and taking pictures. Damn, no wonder some of these reality stars were getting some big egos. If I were treated like that all the time I'd probably be full of myself too. The Z-listers were all getting treated like A-listers. It was nuts.

The party went off without a hitch this time. There were even more celebrity guests at the VIP party, including race car driver Helio Castroneves, legendary singers Salt 'N Pepa, and actors Jonathan Silverman and Jennifer Coolidge (best known as Stifler's mom from the *American Pie* movies). Salt 'N Pepa were actually in production for their own new reality show that was filming them during the Mardi Gras experience. There were several cameras rolling, and I did my best to try to get myself a cameo.

The Krewe of Bacchus parade was approaching, and the annual tradition of the celebrity monarchs toasting each other was about to be celebrated. Accordingly, everyone on our VIP balcony was getting their champagne glasses filled. As the waiters came around with full bottles, I sensed an opportunity, and asked one of the waiters if I could help them pour. He gladly let me take a bottle off his hands.

I made a beeline for the front of the balcony, where Salt 'N Pepa were talking with Helio Castroneves, while two cameras filmed for Salt 'N Pepa's reality show. Luckily, they all had empty glasses.

"Can I fill you guys up?" I asked as I positioned myself within view of the camera.

"Yes please!" they all said. "Thanks!"

I poured the expensive champagne into each of their glasses, with the bright light shining on us from the film crew. This scene has to make it to the final cut, I thought, and congratulated myself for my cleverness.

And it did! When the show aired months later on VH1, there it was, the Orpheus party scene, and my 15 seconds of fame! Unfortunately, it was just my hand that got the fame. There was a close-up on my hand pouring the champagne into all of their glasses, and then the camera pulled back to Helio and Salt 'N Pepa talking away. My face was nowhere to be seen. Oh well.

Anyway, the big celebrity toast—this year made by Bacchus monarch Val Kilmer—went off smoothly. There was no Isaac mic grab. Everyone was happy and we had a great time at the party. It got even better the next day when we met at the convention center for the parade. They were holding a press conference where all of the celebrities in the parade talked about how excited they were to be a part of Orpheus.

We were brought to our own private dressing room to prepare for the press conference. It was full of food and drinks, and it was right next door to the dressing room of another big celebrity in that year's parade—the legendary Joan Rivers. She missed the party the night before, so this was our first chance to talk to her. She was super-nice to us, and Kenny and Evan declared how much they loved her and asked for a picture with her. I don't think she had any idea who Kenny and Evan were, but she graciously took the picture and told us how happy she was to be there.

Evan and Kenny with Joan Rivers right before the parade started

After she left the six of us hung out in our dressing room for a while, commenting about how insane this all was. We were alongside many A-listers, and getting equal treatment. Was this the pinnacle of all pinnacles?

"What should we say at the press conference?" Dunbar asked me.

"Just talk about how great the tradition of Mardi Gras is, how New Orleans is an amazing city, and how wonderful Orpheus is. Be positive, brief and polite."

When it was time to go on, we were escorted down the hall by several security guards dressed in tuxedos with mics in their ears. It was so cool having an assigned security detail; and this was *real* security, not Mario the Bobo-hunter. Kenny, Evan and Dunbar did well during the press conference as the rest of us stood in the back to watch. After the press conference was over, we were escorted again by security over to our float.

"Holy shit!" I said. "It's the Smokey Mary!"

The Smokey Mary Train is the first float of the entire Orpheus parade. Last year we were placed somewhere in the middle where Isaac could blend in. But now we were front and center, with our train car labeled "MTV's Reality Star Cast." It was awesome.

We climbed aboard in our Orpheus Mardi Gras costumes and looked at all of the beads and other "throws" stocked up to give out to the crowds. We could barely move standing on the top of the train with so many things to toss.

The parade slowly worked its way down the streets of New Orleans en route to the official starting point in the Garden District. Before reaching that point, an annual tradition is to stop at some of the back streets so that everyone can get off the floats and sample the drinks and eats at some legendary local bars. After about an hour of hanging out it's time to jump back on the float and get rolling again. No worries about finishing the drinks, though; not only could we bring any bar drinks with us, but the float itself was stocked with endless alcohol. Since it was late afternoon and the parade would last for about 6 hours, there would most certainly be a lot of drinking and bead-throwing to come.

Before we knew it the parade was on its way, and thousands of parade goers were screaming for freebies to be thrown from our float. Many went wild when they saw Kenny, Evan and Dunbar. It was mayhem, but a good mayhem.

At the top of the Garden District there were lots of families with kids, and we'd throw out a lot of stuffed animals to them. But as we worked our way slowly down St Charles Avenue the crowd grew less and less family-friendly and more and more wild-and-rowdy. By the time we arrived downtown on Canal Street, it was complete debauchery. Girls everywhere flashing their bobos, cheering the reality stars and screaming for the best beads we had. The alcohol kept flowing and we kept throwing. The six hours went by like 20 minutes. It was non-stop craziness, impossible to describe, impossible to forget.

The parade ended back at the New Orleans Convention Center, riding right into Orpheuscapade, the annual huge ball with bands, singers, and 3,000 attendees who paid good money to be a part of the festivities. Each float gets announced as it enters, so when we rolled passed the main music stage of the ballroom, the MC announced our presence:

"And on the Smokey Mary Train we have members of MTV's Reality Star Cast: Kenny, Evan and Dunbar!"

The crowd cheered. We waved and tossed out all the remaining throws from the float, in one last orgiastic purge. As the float parked and we got off to join the partying, we couldn't stop talking about how surreal it all was.

"Holy shit!" Kenny shouted.

"Insane!" Evan agreed.

"This year was even better than last year!" Dunbar exclaimed.

"So many bobos!" Mario grinned blissfully.

"Thanks so much for letting me be a part of this!" Justin said.

"Great crew, great experience!" I summed it up. "Glad to share this with all of you crazy guys!"

We kept drinking, dancing, meeting fans and partying the night away. New Orleans Mardi Gras 2009 was one for the record books. It felt as if we had officially arrived into stardom. I had been part of some amazing celebrity VIP experiences over the years, but this one blew them all away. For one weekend, we were equals with the A-listers! Even if it wasn't long lived.

Dunbar, Andy, Kenny, Mario, and Evan celebrating during Mardi Gras

CHAPTER 9

THE Z-GIRLS

If I've been dwelling overmuch on my experiences with the male cast members of reality shows, it's because frankly they were the most fun. Hanging out with these guys while they were partying with gorgeous girls and soaking up the applause and the booze provided me with some of the most memorable experiences of my life, and even the not-so-great experiences gave me something to look back at and laugh. I kept thinking how it would all make a great book someday.

But while the guys have been hogging the spotlight so far, let's not forget the Z-list ladies who were adding a different perspective to my roster. Veronica and Rachel started it all for me, of course. And even though as a single guy I loved the appearances with the "hot guy" cast members, who in turn attracted all the hot females, I still followed the dollar signs. And here was the reality: the club owners—usually men—who were paying for the appearances, were sometimes more interested in booking (and hanging with) a hot female cast member. Which was a bit absurd: did these small-town middle-aged Casanovas really think they stood a chance with the goddesses of MTV? Nor was this an especially wise business practice; the male Z-listers usually drew bigger crowds of female fans, which in turn drew bigger crowds of guys looking for action. The female Z-listers just didn't always have the same drawing power; but who was I to turn down an appearance when I was being offered good money to do so?

That's how I ended up booking the stunningly gorgeous Shauvon Torres, who originally starred in *Real World: Sydney* with the unholy trio of Isaac, Cohutta and Dunbar. The owner of a club in Connecticut had just watched some episodes, and he really wanted to meet her. He gave me a call and requested Shauvon and Trisha Cummings, both very hot girls from that season, for an appearance at his club.

The cool thing was, the Sydney season of *Real World* had just come out, and the girls had never done an appearance before. So when I called to offer them the gig, they jumped at it. Things had really come full circle for me. When I first started out, Veronica and Rachel had to explain every aspect of the business to me. Now I was showing the ropes to new cast members, fresh on the scene.

I negotiated the contract as usual—a three-hour appearance with transportation, hotels, drinks, meals included. The girls were flying in, so I planned to meet them at the hotel. When I arrived they were already there in the lobby, and SHIT, television did not do them justice. Yes, I was expecting two blonde bombshells, but in person, Wow! I was actually speechless for a moment when they introduced themselves. But I quickly regained my composure.

"Awesome to meet you lovely ladies," I said smoothly. "So this is your first gig?"

"Yeah, it is, and we're so excited," Shauvon said.

"Tell us what to expect, Andy," Trisha added.

I gave them a quick rundown of what to expect: the DJ booth, the VIP area, the posing for pictures, maybe hosting a contest or pouring shots...

"Sounds like a good time to me," Trisha said.

"Can't beat getting paid to party," said Shauvon.

I agreed.

The three of us hung out and had some drinks in my room beforehand, getting to know each other. Gotta say, in all my teenage fantasies, I never imagined I'd be sitting in a hotel room with two incredibly beautiful TV stars all to myself. But as I kept telling myself, it's all business. Keep it professional.

At 10 pm I got the text that our ride was waiting and we all headed downstairs. To my relief, it wasn't a shitty heap with gross food wrappers in the backseat, but instead a nice clean Town Car. This was a sign of things to come: for some reason everything went ultra-smooth at this event. There were no annoying obnoxious fans or mean staff members. Everyone was great to us, and kept handing us drinks before we even had to ask. The crowd was huge and the Z-girls were loving it. The fact that everything was going so perfect made me look like a hero.

"Andy, this is the best!" Shauvon shouted to me in between beats of dance music. "I hope you keep booking me and Trisha. We wanna do all our events with you!"

I liked the sound of that.

The owner paid us, and we were driven back to the hotel. All in all, an uneventful appearance; we were treated great and everything went perfectly. And if it wasn't for what happened next, you wouldn't even be hearing about this night.

"Do you guys wanna have a few more drinks?" Trisha asked as we thanked the driver and walked back into the hotel.

"I'm always down for more drinks," I responded.

"Same here," Shauvon added.

So the three of us went back up to my room and I poured us drinks. We talked about how fun the night was, and Shauvon and Trisha kept saying how they wanted to do more awesome events like this one. I was definitely feeling cool, the hip agent helping these new hot reality stars find their way to the good paying appearances.

We put the television on while we drank, and I flipped to MTV. Sure enough, they were airing repeats of *Real World Sydney*. Now I really started to feel my ego swell—I was sitting on my hotel bed having drinks with two of the hottest reality stars at the time, and then turning to the TV set and seeing them right there on their own show. It was weird and surreal. But amazing.

Then it got a little more surreal. I noticed that Shauvon seemed to be getting closer and closer to me on the bed. Was she just getting tired, leaning towards me sleepily? Or was I just imagining it all?

All of a sudden her hand was on my leg. This was not my imagination. This was Shauvon making a move.

Okay Andy, my brain told me, be professional. Get off the bed. Stand up and pour another drink. This is not cool. Don't let yourself cross the agent/ client line. You'll regret this tomorrow.

Yeah, my brain was making perfect sense to me. But, on the other hand, this was the hottest girl on reality TV, and *she* seemed fine with crossing the line. And frankly I didn't care what I'd regret tomorrow, I was thinking about tonight…

So I decided to listen to my other brain. I leaned in for a kiss, and she leaned in too, and—it happened. We started making out!

I couldn't believe what was happening. This was a lot different from hanging out with my male clients! And yes, I was mad at myself for crossing that agent/client business line, but this could've been my only chance to ever fool around with a stunning reality star. I couldn't pass that up. I knew I'd be kicking myself forever if I did. Besides, she was there in front of me on the TV screen, and right next to me at the same time, and philosophically it would have been wrong not to explore this once-in-a-lifetime intersection of life and art.

So we kept making out, and our hands went to various places. If you've seen Shauvon then you know the first two things my hands went to. And damn they felt good. . .!

"Okay guys, I'm gonna head to sleep," Trisha interrupted.

I forgot Trisha was even there! Her voice jolted me out of my erotic fantasia and back to the real world. I quickly pulled my hands away and assumed my most professional demeanor under the circumstances.

"Oh no, you don't have to leave, we can all just chill," I said, half thinking that I should stop making out with Shauvon in front of another client, and half imagining that if Trisha stayed she might want to join in (hey, a man can dream).

"No it's cool," said Trisha, "I'm tired anyway. Thanks for an amazing night, Andy. I'll see you in the morning."

"Goodnight Trisha!" Shauvon and I both said.

Trisha left the room, and Shauvon and I resumed making out. My hands went back to Position One, and…well, I'll spare you the specific details. Suffice it to say, a good time was had by all.

But it was just a one-off, and we never followed up in the future. Nor did I make it a habit with the other girls on my roster. That was the one and only time I ever crossed the client/agent line. And no, I don't regret it.

Not all of my female reality star events went as well as Shauvon and Trisha's. And not all of the female Z-listers were as great as they were. Some, in fact, could be just as much of a pain as their male counterparts.

I was doing a nightclub event with Parisa Montazaran, who was also from *Real World: Sydney*; and her co-star Isaac Stout was with us for this one. It was my first time doing an event with Parisa; and Isaac, as we all know, is prone to misbehave. So I was apprehensive about it all, but as always I wasn't going to turn down good money. I figured I'd give it a shot and see how it went.

As usual, we were getting hooked up with drinks in a VIP area and the fans were all over the place. Things seemed to be going okay, and to my relief Isaac and Parisa were getting along great with the club owner. In fact, he liked Isaac and Parisa so much that he told us all to stick around after the bar closed. "We shut down at 2 am and kick everyone out. But you guys are awesome. Want to hang out and party after with me and some of the other staff?" he asked us.

"Hell yeah!" Isaac answered. "Always down to keep partying and drinking."

"We'd be happy to hang out here longer with you guys," Parisa added.

"If they're in, I'm in," I said.

"Perfect, just stay here in the VIP area and I'll bring over two cases of beer."

At 2 am the lights came on and the bouncers ushered everyone out of the bar. We kept drinking in our area, and some staff came over to join us when the owner brought over the two cases of beer.

"You sure it's okay to be partying in here after hours? Is it allowed in this city?" I asked.

The owner laughed. "No, of course it's not allowed. But you can't see in any windows in here, and it's only about ten of us. As long as we aren't loud and obnoxious the cops won't notice. We'll be fine."

That settled, the ten of us cracked open beers and shot the shit for a while.

I didn't notice, but Isaac and Parisa were downing their beers a lot quicker than the others. And their voices were getting a little louder than the owner was comfortable with.

"Just keep it down a little, guys, don't want the cops to know we're still partying in here," he said.

"No problem, we'll keep it calm," I assured him, while looking pointedly at Parisa and Isaac.

But as usual, Isaac wasn't really paying any heed to my words of caution. A minute later he took two bottles from the case of beer, shook them up as much as he could, opened them up and sprayed the contents everywhere. He thought this was funny.

"What the fuck, Isaac?!" I yelled at him (it seems like I was always yelling "what the fuck!" at Isaac), while the owner walked away, clearly pissed, to get some things to clean up the mess.

"Are you serious, dude?" I continued. "The owner's letting us party in here after hours, and this is how you repay his generosity? He just asked you to keep it down, didn't he?"

"Relax, Andy," he said.

There he went again, just telling me to relax and not worrying about any consequences.

"Relax, my ass! You're going to fuck up everything for everybody!"

"Andy!" Parisa interrupted me. I stopped and looked at her in surprise. "Isaac," she explained to me, "can do whatever the fuck he wants. We both can. We're major stars on *The Real World*—you know, the *hottest* show on reality TV! This owner is lucky as fuck that we're even here!"

I couldn't believe what I was hearing.

"The *owner* is lucky??" I said while still in shock. "No, it's more like *you're* lucky that he's paying you to be here and letting you stay after the bar closed. I got news for you—you're not an A-list celebrity, and you can't just go act any way you want. If this is how you're gonna treat bars and their owners, and *me*, then I won't work with you guys again. Simple as that!"

My rant was done. Hers wasn't.

"Not how it works, Andy. If you don't treat us the way we wanna be treated, then we won't work with this bar, this owner, or *you* again," Parisa said.

At that point I was completely okay with that. But not wanting to engage in this argument further, I just shook my head, and walked away to find the owner. I apologized to him for my client's behavior and attitude. "This is not how I like to do business," I assured him.

"It's okay, Andy," he said. "I've seen it all owning a bar. Definitely dealt with worse. I'll still work with you on other gigs. You were nothing but professional."

That was good to hear.

I thanked him again and got Isaac and Parisa the hell out of there. When we got back to the hotel, I said a quick goodbye to them, and went straight to my room. I wasn't going to argue with them again because the chances were slim that I'd work with them again. But it proved my point that female Z-listers can be just as self-centered as the male variety. And when you put two of these winners together on the same night, the combination can be lethal.

I can't leave the Z-girls without mentioning Paula Meronek. Paula first starred on *Real World: Key West,* and she appeared on many *Challenges* after that. She was good-looking but for some reason seemed to have low self-esteem. It was famously documented on her TV show about how she suffered from an eating disorder. Fortunately she won that battle; but during my times with her I could always tell how much she wanted to be accepted by her fellow cast members and her fans. It seemed like a deep-seated insecurity she couldn't quite shake.

But she was a great client. She was always very nice to me and always showed up on time for our events.

And, she was more like the fellow guy cast members than the other Z-girls. Especially when it came to hooking up with fans. Maybe a double standard, but it's commonplace for one of the guy Z-listers to hook up with a random fan after an appearance night. Not so commonplace with the Z-girls.

Except for Paula.

I was doing a college event with both Paula and Mr. Beautiful himself, Kenny Santucci. We were getting $7,500 to participate in a "Singled Out" style game show for the students. I had met their student event booker at a NACA conference, and she came up with the idea. She also said I had the voice of a host so she wanted me to emcee the event.

Awesome. I'd get to be back on stage and finally in the spotlight again.

"Singled Out" was a popular game show from the late 90s on MTV, hosted by Chris Hardwick and Jenny McCarthy. One main contestant would get to pick from 50 singles of the opposite sex, without seeing them, based on the answers they gave to various (usually humorous) questions. In a process of elimination, the field was eventually narrowed down to one person. Then that person would be revealed to the main contestant and they'd go on a date. Pretty simple and straightforward.

The student event leader had wanted to bring this concept back and do a modified version on her campus. In her version, a group of girls (pre-selected by the campus) would get to compete in the Singled Out game for a date with Kenny. And a group of guys would compete for a date with Paula. The winners would come out with us afterwards for a "date."

I was driving Kenny in, and Paula was being driven by Mario, who had once again jumped at the chance to be a our "security" for a reality star event, in the hopes of being paid in bobos. Because we got held up in traffic, we arrived at the hotel at the exact time the college mini-van was there to pick us up. So we checked in hurriedly and came right back downstairs.

But Kenny wasn't ready just yet. "Let's get a drink at the hotel bar before we head over," he suggested to us.

"Dude, they're already here to pick us up, we gotta go."

Kenny was adamant. "I need a drink before I get stuck playing this game. For some reason I don't think this date will be as good as the one in Poughkeepsie," he added.

"Good point," I conceded. "Plus I could use a drink before I have to get on stage and host this thing."

Mario and Paula were both happy to get a drink as well. So we went over to the bar and all had a quick libation. I could see the annoyance on the faces of the students who were there to pick us up. We were already cutting it close on time, and they didn't think we should be drinking before the event.

Oh well.

We drank up quickly and hopped in the typical college-logo-embroidered mini-van and were driven over to the campus. Pleasantries and introductions were exchanged, as was our check for $7,500. Once I had that in hand, it was show time!

I killed it as host, if I do say so myself. I was smooth and funny and the crowd was into it. Kenny went first in the game, and they had him facing the opposite way so that he couldn't see any of the contestants. As we narrowed down the girls, Kenny kept looking at me for hints of how it was going.

He wasn't getting any from me.

The final contestant who won the date with him ended up being a decent-looking girl. Kenny was pleasantly surprised, since he was expecting the worst (as usual). So my guess was he'd end up hooking up with her after the group date that night.

Then it was Paula's turn. I went through the hosting motions again as Paula narrowed down the college student guys on stage until the final winner was determined. He was an 18 year-old freshman, and when he was revealed to the older Paula, she seemed very pleased and gave him a big hug. Damn, how come I never got that lucky when I was 18 years old?

The girl in charge came over and thanked me for my awesome hosting job (thank you very much) and for helping to put on the event. But I give her all the credit. Being a college student leader and putting on these kind of events is challenging and demanding, and it provides major management experience that will help these kids in the real world (no pun intended) way more than many things they can learn in the classroom. If you're reading this and still in college, definitely join your student activities or events/programming board!

After the event we all went on our big group date to dinner and to the bars. It was a fun time and the drinks were flowing—but they weren't free. No college will pay for drinks, so, unlike our nightclub events, the drinks were on us. That didn't stop the grown-ups—me, Mario, Kenny and Paula—from drinking a lot. Paula's date was under-age, so he kept getting big X's on his hand at every bar we went to.

But as Paula kept drinking she kept hanging on her young friend more and more. The next thing I knew, they were making out in front of everyone. Even before Kenny and his date started going at it.

A few hours later it was time for the group date to end, and for our ride to bring us back to our hotel. As we pulled in front I thanked the student in charge again and we all said our goodbyes.

"You coming with?" Kenny asked his date as he stepped out of the car.

"Sure, if you want me to," she said.

"Of course I do, beautiful." I told you, I saw that coming. Kenny Santucci never disappoints.

Not to be out-done. Paula held her hand out to the 18-year-old. "And what about you, sweetie? Are you coming with me?" she asked.

Total surprise filled the young guy's face. "Really?" he asked. "I can?"

"Definitely, let's have some fun." Paula said.

"Fuck yeah!" the dude shouted.

I rolled my eyes.

Kenny and his hot date went to his room, Paula and her young date went to her room, and Mario and I went to my room. I didn't have an extra room that night so we were sharing.

So Kenny and Paula would be enjoying the extra-curricular reality star perks, while I'd be enjoying the sweet sound of Mario's sonorous sinuses, as he snored away like a bulldozer.

Oh well.

Yes, the Z-girls of *Real World* and *The Challenge* were highly entertaining in their own right, and while I might prefer partying with the male contingent, I can't say these ladies didn't add mightily to the craziness of my roster-building years. Even though I don't still work with all of them—some for very good reasons—I definitely have no regrets about my money-making experiences with them.

CHAPTER 10
CAN DO NO WRONG

HERE'S THE THING ABOUT THE TV reality world: by its very definition, it takes place in reality. Virtually any ordinary schlump off the street (probably with good pecs or bountiful bobos) can become a reality star. The bar is not high. In fact, there's some question if there's a bar at all. The standards are so low that you can basically step right over them.

But that doesn't mean that *everyone* can be a reality star. It's not an open call: some people make the cut, due to personality or luck or p.r. savvy, and some people don't even get out of the gate. You have to be, for lack of a better word, interesting. And most people aren't.

But that doesn't stop the wannabes from dreaming. And as my tenure in the agent business progressed, I started getting more and more calls from people who aspired to Z-list superstardom, and wanted to know if I could get them on a show.

That included good ole Justin, who tagged along on my legendary Mardi Gras experience with Dunbar, Kenny and Evan. After Justin got a little taste of the reality celebrity experience, he became a man with a mission: and the mission was to get on a show himself.

"Dude, come on, help me get cast!" he would say to me all the time.

"How many times do I have to tell you, Justin?—I don't do casting. But if you ever make it on a show, I'll get you paid for appearances. That I promise."

A few months later it was announced nationwide that in honor of the 20th season of *The Real World,* the show producers would only be casting six of the seven housemates. The seventh member would be voted on and chosen by viewers in an online contest.

I sent Justin a link to the article and told him this was his big chance.

Not really. It was a nice PR gimmick, but tens of thousands of people from all over the country would be submitting their photos and videos online to the casting contest webpage. The odds that Justin would even make it past the first round were remote at best.

But that didn't stop him. He wanted to win that 7th spot, and he was willing to go to any extreme to make it happen. To that end, he hired a professional photographer to take some publicity shots. Something to entice the ladies. Now Justin is a good guy, but he's also 5"6" and bald. Not a world-beater. How do you make that enticing? Well, the photographer decided to go for broke: he had Justin take his shirt off and pose in ridiculous Fabio-style sexy positions. Justin had a good physique for his size, but nevertheless these pictures were just hilarious. Unfortunately he wouldn't let me put them in this book, but I bet you could find them online somewhere if you looked hard enough.

Armed with his embarrassing photos, Justin spent every waking hour trying to get people to vote for him, and I admired his relentless if ill-conceived determination. As the final month of the contest was upon us, he called me one afternoon, screaming, "Check out the website!"

"Why?"

"Just check it out!"

"I'm pretty busy right now. Just tell me."

"I'm in the top 20! Can you fucking believe it?!"

No, I couldn't believe it. "*You're* in the top 20? Are you shitting me?"

"No! Dude, I'm less than 20 away from getting on *The Real World*!"

How could he be in the Top 20? With those pictures? "Are you sure you're reading it right? It's not the bottom 20?"

"Don't break my balls. I'm telling ya, man! I'm knocking on the door!"

I guess stranger things had happened. "Hey, that's great. You know I'm rooting for you."

To his credit, Justin could sense a golden opportunity here, and he wasn't going to let it pass. "Is there anything you can do to help me out? Come on, man, you got connections. Have the current cast members tell people to vote for me."

"Can't, dude, they aren't supposed to pick favorites. Just keep doing what you're doing. It's obviously working."

"Well—do you have any event coming up that I can come to?"

I wasn't crazy about that idea. I didn't want him horning in on a client's gig and causing extra anxiety, stress and aggravation just to promote his own campaign. Besides, there wasn't an event within driving distance in the next few weeks anyway. But then I thought of something.

"I'll call you back in a few." I said and hung up quick.

I had noticed that some of the clubs I was working with were getting cheaper and cheaper. They were either trying to pay less for a Z-lister than the agreed-upon minimum, or they were booking fewer events. So, I had an idea. It was a longshot, but maybe they would book my good friend Justin, a top 20 *Real World* finalist. Sure, he was unknown, but he was listed on the contest website, and he'd cost a lot less.

Would any club go for it?

The answer was, shockingly, yes.

Dewey of Club Alchemy in New Haven (where, you'll recall,

Wes and Johanna hosted the infamous Sexual Position contest) was interested. In fact, we made a deal that same day.

Was this really happening? Did I just book my friend, who had never been on a reality show, who was only a finalist in an online contest to potentially be on a reality show—did I just book a complete nobody for an appearance at a nightclub? I sure as hell did.

I was beginning to wonder, what kind of business was I dedicating so much of my life to? It was getting a little over the top, and in not so good ways.

But for now, I was gonna keep rolling with it.

I called Justin. "Okay, so in two weeks I got you booked to host an event at Alchemy in New Haven. You can tell the crowd to vote for you while we host some contests. It's $500, 2 hotel rooms, complimentary dinner and drinks all night. Cool?"

"Don't the reality stars get at least $1500 to show up at a club?" Justin asked.

I wanted to reach through the phone and choke this guy. "You're not a reality star, Justin. You're on a website as a finalist who MIGHT or might NOT get on a show. You're welcome, by the way."

"Okay, okay. Thanks man. Yeah sounds good. I'm in."

"I already told the club you're in. If you weren't in, after all this shit you've done to get votes, I wouldn't be talking to you anymore."

I hoped I wasn't going to regret this.

I had a gig in New York City the night before the event, so Justin would have to meet me in New Haven. Luckily our other friend Hunter, a loud guy who was fun to be around as long as it was in small doses, really wanted to come to the gig.

"Yo Binder," he said when he called the night before. "Let me come tomorrow, I'll drive Justin. He can even pick which one of my two Porsches I take." Hunter made good money as a medical device salesman, and he never got tired of informing you of the fact.

"You don't need to remind me you have two Porsches, dude, I know."

"Well, do you have any?"

"No I don't."

"There you go. Didn't think so."

Another guy who needed a smack. "Okay, you can bring Justin as long as you behave at the gig."

"I always behave. But I am gonna try to catch a blow."

"Catch a blow? Look, no cocaine around us, keep it to yourself."

"No man, a blow job. I'm sure there'll be a chick there to blow me."

Mario with the bobos. Hunter with the blows. I had some classy friends.

"Just pick up Justin at 5 pm and I'll meet you guys at the hotel around 8."

"Nice, Binder, see you then."

That evening while I was making the boring solo drive up from NYC to New Haven, Hunter called.

"I'm with the talent," he announced dramatically. "He is present and accounted for. I made sure he's sufficiently hydrated, and now he's sitting comfortably in the passenger seat of my Porsche, resting up for his showbiz debut on stage at Alchemy tonight."

"Glad to see you're taking your responsibilities very seriously, Hunter," I said jokingly. "I hope Justin is appreciating the service."

"He is, indeed. He told me he'd make it up to me later."

Hmmm.

We all arrived around the same time at the 5-star hotel that I had somehow procured for my non-reality star less-than-Z-lister friend. And of course we performed the usual ritual of hotel room drinks before the gig.

While we drank, I opened my laptop and pulled up the updated website for Club Alchemy from that day. I was hoping there would be a mention of Justin's appearance.

The main page featured one picture only. It was a huge photo of a shirtless Justin posing in a failed attempt to be sexy; underneath was the caption "Vote for Me for Real World 20! Appearing Live Tonight at Alchemy!"

"Holy shit, look at this!" I said, laughing out loud. I knew it would have been more respectful to my "client" to keep a straight face, but I couldn't help it. Plus, let's be real. He wasn't really a client.

The other two gathered around the screen, and Hunter burst out laughing. "I'm supposed to vote for *that?*" he exclaimed.

Even Justin laughed sheepishly. He had to admit how goofy it looked.

The three of us were doubled over in the hotel room, laughing uncontrollably. We couldn't stop. I had tears running down my cheeks, I was laughing so hard.

And maybe I was laughing a bit at myself, and crying, too. To think that this is what it had come to: booking a wannabe reality star for $500. Would it all go downhill from here? I hoped not. Either way, at least it was hilarious as fuck.

A club staffer picked us up and brought us over to the club, and as soon as we got there my man Justin was recognized by the crowd.

"Ohmygod! You're the guy from the website! Let me get a picture with you!" said girl after girl after girl.

Again, what the fuck? Seemed like in this day and age all you had to do was put your picture online in some contest and the fans came flocking.

Justin was loving the attention, taking pictures with dozens of girls, flirting away, telling everyone, in what was to become his favorite trademark term, that he's a "fun-lovin' party guy."

And he was loving meeting all those fun-lovin' party girls.

Justin had heard about the Sexual Position contest we did with Wes and Johanna at this very same club, and he loved the idea. Now that he was the "star talent", he really wanted to host a new version.

Dewey had no problem with this; it was a hit before, so why not bring it back? I wasn't so optimistic. Who was going to get down and dirty on stage for the likes of this total nobody? I suspected it would lay an egg and put a damper on the whole evening.

And again, I was wrong. We had to turn away contestants. And it was just as wild as it was with Wes and Johanna. I was dumbfounded. I couldn't believe what people would do for this unknown host. But I had to admit, he did sound like a natural in front of a mic.

"Okay, everyone, don't forget to vote for me, your boy Justin, for *Real World 20*! DJ! Play that music for our sexy couple number 1 and let's see how wild they can get for us!"

The crowd cheered, the music blared, and the couple got VERY wild. Justin proved to be highly skilled at whipping up the energy. He might have been even a little better than Wes with the crowd hype.

Hunter and I stood to the side of the stage, a few feet away from Justin. As the "star talent" went down the line with the couples, Hunter leaned over towards him.

"You said you'd return the favor for the Porsche. Remember?" Hunter yelled over the music.

Justin nodded in rhythm. "Just tell me what you want, dude," he said in between the music beats and the wild dancing on stage.

"Tell everyone I'm on a reality show," said Hunter. "I want the girls flocking to me like they're flocking to you."

"You got it," said Justin, cocking his finger at him as if he were Frank Sinatra promising him a swinging night.

The contest ended with the crowd voting vocally for the craziest, wildest couple, and that gave Justin one more chance to promote himself.

"You guys love me, right?" The crowd cheered in affirmation. "Then don't forget, go online and vote for me to be on the next season of *Real World!*" More cheers. I was still amazed. For one night, for 2,000 fans, this guy really was a star.

"I wanna thank my friend and agent Andy for setting this up tonight. Andy! Wave to the crowd!"

I waved.

"And," he continued, "I wanna thank another one of my friends for coming out tonight. Ladies and Gentlemen, say hello to the ONE MILLION DOLLAR winner of the upcoming season of *Amazing Race*, Hunter!" Justin smoothly lied.

I looked at Hunter. "One million dollars?"

Hunter grinned. "Not bad, huh?"

"Say hi to the crowd, Hunter!" Justin exhorted him.

Hunter happily grabbed the mic and took center stage. "Hey, New Haven! I'm here to party with you all night long!"

The crowd cheered again.

I felt like I was witnessing a fundamental shift in the paradigm. Now we had two nobodies on stage getting cheered for being nobodies. What the fuck was going on?

We walked off stage and into the masses. Girls started throwing themselves at Justin. At one point he had his arms around four girls, making out with all four of them at once, while Hunter and I watched in disbelief.

"Is this really happening?" I asked.

"He's so fish," Hunter said.

"Fish?"

"Yeah, selfish. Fish as fuck. Not sharing the wealth. Justin! You're fish!"

Justin ignored him and continued his attention to the girls.

But Hunter wasn't alone for long. A minute later a really unattractive girl—sorry, but she was truly unsightly, maybe a 202—came up to him. "Hey! You're the million-dollar winner, aren't you?"

"Yes I am," he said confidently.

"I'm Pam. Wanna hook up?"

What was my life coming to?

"I do," Hunter said, and then he leaned over to me. "Gonna catch that blow. See you later."

I guess a blow is a blow. Still, I couldn't help feeling that I had stumbled into an alternate universe.

The rest of the night a few girls came over to me, and I had some fun. Hey, I was the agent of a non-reality star, I must've been cool somehow to these people.

Afterwards we went back to the hotel. I let Justin have his own room, since he was the "talent" of the night, and he brought several girls from the club back with him. Which further amazed me, because they'd already seen his 'attempt at sexy' posed photos, they knew what they were getting.

Being a conservative kind of guy (depending on the night), I went back with just one girl, who was way better-looking than Hunter's, by the way. I was sharing the room with Hunter—he was already passed out with 202 on his bed when we got there.

My girl left before I feel asleep. But when I woke up in the morning, 202 was still there with Hunter. We needed to get ready, and I wanted her out of there, so I hinted to Hunter to get rid of her. "Yeah, so we better pull it together," I said, getting out of bed. "We all have to hit the road soon."

Hunter got the hint and turned to his girl. He hadn't forgotten that he was a million-dollar *Amazing Race* winner, so he adroitly kept the fantasy going. "Listen babe," he said to her, "I gotta fly out in a few hours for a radio interview in Puerto Rico. But it's been fun. Maybe see you again sometime."

"Oooo, Puerto Rico? So jealous! That's amazing."

"Yeah, I know. Comes with being a celebrity. I *am* pretty amazing." And from a certain standpoint, he was.

After Miss 202 left, I burst out laughing. "You seriously hooked up with her?" I asked Hunter.

"I told you I wanted to catch a blow."

"Don't you have any standards?"

"Not for a blowjob, no."

"You gotta admit, man, that girl looked like an ogre."

"Ogre me!" Hunter responded.

And from that point on, whenever either of us wanted to hook up with an ugly girl, we always shouted—"Ogre me!"

Later that morning we all went to a nearby diner for breakfast and a recap of the night. Justin and Hunter were hung over but still enjoying the memory of their conquests. As for me, I still couldn't believe I had booked Justin for this event. He wasn't even on a show! And it was still just as wild as some of my events with Wes, or Kenny or Landon. It truly baffled me. How did things take such a strange turn? What was this world's obsession with fame? I didn't know, and for the moment I tried not to care. I was still enjoying the ride.

We said our goodbyes and agreed that we had to do this again sometime soon—maybe when our top 20 finalist was finally chosen number 1! With this kind of enthusiasm, how could he lose?

Well, he did lose, unfortunately. Poor Justin never got his shot as a reality star. And we never did an event like that with him again. But I don't think anyone else in the country can say they got to host a crazy club event just because they were almost cast in a reality show. A surreal life indeed.

Things were pretty huge for me at this point, and it wasn't slowing down one bit. I felt like I could do no wrong. Having become associated with reality TV on some subliminal level, I was getting a little renown, even a small degree of fame, and fully enjoying the benefits of it.

This couldn't be better illustrated than by an incident that happened at a club appearance with Shane Landrum from *Road Rules* and *The Challenge*. Shane, one of the nicer reality stars I worked with, was openly gay, so needless to say he appealed to a different fan base than the usual male stars. Not that there weren't plenty of girls there basking in the glow of his looks and his celebrity, and I'm sure a few of them secretly hoped they could turn him to their side. But the vibe in general was definitely more, shall we say, flamboyant.

My friend Gavin was with me, as well as his sister and two of her friends from college, and we were having a blast. Shane was friendly as hell, and the fans loved him. He was also clearly hitting on Gavin, and we were all getting a kick out of that.

"Shane, I'm not into guys, sorry," Gavin said, as we all played beer pong at the club.

"Can't be sure until you try," Shane jokingly responded.

Gavin was more interested in one of his sister's friends. I actually had my eye on her myself, but she was giving Gavin more attention. Didn't she know I was a reality-star agent? Oh, well.

Now when we first arrived in town we were running late so I had to drive straight to the club. I figured when the gig was over we would get shuttled back to the hotel and I would pick up my car in the morning. But at the end of the night the owner was nowhere to be seen, and we were stuck without a ride. And everyone was complaining about wanting to get back to the hotel. So...

"You know, fuck it—it's less than a mile down the road, I'll just drive us over there," I brilliantly decided, after we had had free drinks all night.

We stumbled out of the club and over to my car. I got in the driver's seat, Gavin in the passenger seat, and Shane and the three girls squeezed in the back.

"Let's do it," I said, and threw it in reverse. I smoothly backed out of the spot and BANG!

Shit, what was that?

"Oh fuck!" I yelled. "I hit the parked car behind me! I'm so screwed!"

"Hold on," Gavin said, and got out of the car. He came back thirty seconds later. "No damage at all, you're fine."

I breathed a sigh of relief and put the car back into drive.

Before I could even move, all of a sudden there were flashing lights in front of me. A police car had pulled right over to us—it must have been sitting in the parking lot. Now two officers were getting out.

Shit, really screwed now.

"Quick, put a penny in your mouth!" Shane told me. "It gets rid of any alcohol breath."

Never heard that one before, but I quickly complied, hoping upon hope that there was even a small chance it would work.

One cop went over to Gavin's window and the other came to mine.

"License and registration," he said very seriously.

"Here you go sir," I responded, sliding the penny in my mouth to one side so he wouldn't see it. "Sorry about that, we were just leaving an event at the club."

"And you've been drinking tonight?"

I wasn't going to deny the obvious. "I have had a few."

"More than a few, I think. The smell of alcohol coming from this car is pretty overpowering," the officer said. "What event are you talking about?"

Time to flash my credentials and hope for the best. "So I'm an agent for MTV reality stars and we have Shane Landrum from *Road Rules* and *The Challenge* in the car." I pointed back to Shane. The officer didn't bother to look. "We did a paid appearance at the club, and we were just heading back to our hotel for the night. It's the hotel right down the road."

The officer nodded thoughtfully. "Never heard of this MTV show or the person you're taking about."

Shane started laughing from the backseat.

I gave him a dirty look. This is no time to be an asshole, Shane.

"Well, I'm being completely honest with you, officer," I said.

"Give me your keys and everyone sit tight for a few. We'll be back."

I handed him my keys and we all sat very tight while the two officers walked into the club.

"I'm totally fucked," I said numbly.

"Let's just be patient and see what happens," Gavin said.

"Easy for you to say. You're not the one who's fucked, I am."

Everyone remained fairly silent, not wanting to freak me out any more than I already was.

We waited and waited. It was probably about ten minutes, but it seemed like hours. The suspense and anxiety were driving me nuts.

Finally, the two officers emerged from the club. "Here it comes," I thought. "They're gonna slap on the cuffs and haul me away."

At that very moment, I got a text from the club owner:

Andy—you're lucky we have a good relationship with the cops in this town. We take care of them, they take care of us, and we vouched for you and your crew. You're all set.

All set? Off the hook? Not fucked? No way, can't be.

The officer showed up at my window.

"Here are your keys. Drive carefully and have a good night," he said.

And they got in their squad car and left.

WHAT? He just handed me my keys back, and that was it? No ticket, no jail, nothing? I was speechless.

Nobody else in the car was.

"Hell yeah, Andy! Let's go!" Shane shouted.

"Told you not to worry," Gavin said.

"Let's go back to the hotel and keep drinking!" one of the girls said.

Great idea. At this point I needed another drink—or two, or ten. I had already sobered up quicker than I ever had in my life. My heart was racing as I drove about ten miles under the speed limit the half mile back to the hotel, and we made it without incident. Thank God!

The rest of the night consisted of our own private after-party in the hotel room, filled with drinks, nudity, puking, and hooking up. The latter activity only Gavin partook in, but that was okay by me. After the relief of not getting arrested, the rest of the night was a total blast.

SO AGAIN, I HAD THE Z-LIST to thank. I couldn't believe what I could get away with because of who I was with, and what they did. And I appreciated being connected like this—it was like being part of the mob.

But still, I had all kinds of doubts and misgivings bubbling up. Was this what my life was all about? Had I reached the limits of my career? Was there anything more to it than the confined sphere of the Z-list, or was this all there was for me?

CHAPTER 11

JERSEY IS ON THE MAP

IN DECEMBER OF 2009, IN THE height of my Z-list insanity ride, an unlikely phenomenon hit the American scene in the form of a new reality show called *The Jersey Shore*. It wasn't much different from any other slice-of-life reality show, and it followed the tried-and-true *Real World* formula: throw a bunch of hot guys and girls into a living space, turn on the cameras and watch them party and pair up and get on each other's nerves. If a fight or a wedding breaks out, all the better. There were dozens of shows like that on cable, and more coming every season. But for some reason, this one particular drama-thon set in Seaside Heights N.J. struck a chord with everyone, all over the country. People couldn't get enough of these crazy, obnoxious Italian (or fake Italian) kids roaming the boardwalk with their skin and their hormones exposed, and their unforgettable nicknames like "Snooki" and "The Situation."

By the time I paid attention and looked outside of my *Real World, Road Rules* and *The Challenge* cast specialties, and became clued in to the magnitude of the Jersey earthquake, it was basically too late. These guys hit so fast that I never really got a chance to

155

work with the big dogs. In no time at all they had agents, managers, a whole P.R. operation guiding them from one lucrative gig
to the next. And I even had met and partied with Snooki years
before, when she was just another girl from Poughkeepsie! But I
missed the boat with her. She signed with her manager who she still
has today (a great guy by the way). Still, I was already questioning
where this Z-list ride was taking me. And this lack of signing any
Jersey Shore superstars didn't help things.

Kenny with Snooki and Ryder in the VIP area at a nightclub event

So for the time being I had to be content with the leftovers:
the guest stars, the one-season wonders, the wanna-bes, the hang-
ers-on, the crash-and-burners. This was the hard-core Z-list, the
Z-listers that even some Z-listers looked down on.

It wasn't easy finding gigs for the leftovers. They had very
little buzz; nobody seemed to care where they showed up or not.
The best bet was pairing them with a bigger name, to make the
event splashier. They were like the opening acts for a rock band;
you didn't really care if you heard them or not, but you knew at
least you were getting a full show. Of course, it was important to

make sure there was the right chemistry between the components. Otherwise...

Which brings me to Caitlin Ryder. Ryder, as she's commonly known, was Snooki's BFF for years, and because of this she was a frequent guest on *Jersey Shore*. She had just been featured in the premiere of the new season, in which she'd gotten very cozy with DJ Pauly D, one of the most desired guys in the country at the time. Because of their camera-friendly make-out sessions, Ryder became a sensation and part of a national catchphrase. In the words of Pauly D, "Whether you're the first man in or the last man in, Ryder!"

Ryder had appeared in a few episodes in previous seasons of Jersey Shore, but now she was trending worldwide on Twitter's top 10, and becoming a household name.

She was still more of a curiosity than a force, though, and that put her more or less in my wheelhouse. Ryder knew me well from our Poughkeepsie days, when she'd come drink with us at the hotel before our *Real World* cast appearances, and was aware of my extensive experience with booking reality stars. So when she started getting serious attention she asked me to sign her and help her capitalize on her sudden fame. I was happy to do so—she was cute and hot and seemed easy to work with, a very appetizing combination—and the appearances actually started to roll in. I mean if I was able to book Justin, I better be able to book the best friend of the most famous reality star of all time. It's all in the hustle.

It was just a month later when I heard from my old "friend" Sid, a sketchy promoter who had involved me in several dubious undertakings in the past. Sid had a proposal for us: he had already booked Jersey star Deena Cortese to appear at a nightclub upstate, and was advertising the appearance as "Deena plus a Special Guest." So now he needed a special guest, and he wanted Ryder. This wasn't exactly a knockout offer—who wanted to be a surprise "Special Guest" with no billing?—but he was offering Ryder some decent money, and it was hopefully a stepping stone to bigger things.

"Oh, by the way," added Sid, "we'll be stopping at a few more businesses on the way." Typical Sid—I knew damn well that he was getting paid extra for these other stops, while paying us a single fee. It was a given with Sid that he was going to exploit you one way or another. But whatever—we were getting paid and he always hooked us up with a great limo, food and drinks and a good time, so why not?

The gig was back in Rochester, New York. As I've said, Rochester is halfway between Syracuse and Buffalo on the Thruway, and a long drive from anywhere. It was gonna be even longer for Ryder and Mario.

Mario was picking up Ryder from Poughkeepsie on his way to Albany. Mario now lived in New York City, so whenever a cast member needed a private ride to an appearance within a six-hour drive, Mario always jumped at the chance to be of service. It meant more bobo potential. And free drinks. Being an imposing 6'4", it was nice to have Mario around as our "personal bodyguard"; he could scare off some of the wackos, and he made the Z-listers feel that they were being treated with the importance they deserved. Mario was always cool with taking on the security role. But he never really took the role too seriously. He just loved the perks of the reality star gigs, especially the free alcohol and the groupies. Yup, there were groupies even in Rochester.

I met up with Ryder and Mario in Albany, and we drove west from there.

We got to the hotel about four hours later. Sometime after we checked in, Sid met us out front with the limo, and gave us the itinerary for the day, which he had scribbled on a piece of paper. "First we're stopping at a hookah lounge."

"A hookah lounge?" I was amused. "They have hookah lounges in Rochester?"

Sid smiled creepily. "You got no idea what they have in Rochester." He resumed: "Next, we go to a tanning salon, and then to a travel agency at the mall, and then we hit a pizza place, then dinner, then the nightclub." Again, typical Sid, squeezing every spare dollar out of this one-shot deal.

"Where's Deena?" I asked.

"She's meeting us at the hookah lounge. So, ladies and gentlemen," he said, rubbing his hands together with moist enthusiasm, "shall we do this thing?"

The limo delivered us to the hookah lounge and Ryder, Mario and I walked in. Deena was already there in the back. When she spotted us a strange look came over her face, almost as though she were shocked to see us. She managed to work up a smile, and said, "Hi, Ryder," with the kind of classic fake sincerity you hear in schoolgirl cliques. "Hi, Deena," Ryder answered back, just as heartfelt. I sensed a little tension between them, but no more than you'd find when any two reality "stars" have to share the spotlight. Ryder sat on one side of the room with a hookah, and Deena sat on the other, and their fans gathered around, and both ladies were gracious and charming. It couldn't have gone better.

After a while, Sid checked his watch and leaned into my ear. "We should head over to the tanning salon."

We started gathering the troops. But Deena wasn't ready yet. "I'm still busy." Doing what, it wasn't clear. She was just sitting next to the hookah. I guessed she was stalling so she could make her entrance at the tanning salon after Ryder, and get the biggest cheers. Divas. Whatever. Fine with me.

So Ryder, Mario and I took the limo over to the tanning salon. Sid said he'd meet us there with Deena in a few.

In front of the salon, hundreds of fans were lined up, screaming, going wild at our approach. They thought they were getting Deena! When Ryder stepped out, alone, there was a big whoosh of disappointment, a wordless communal "what the fuck?" Some of the fans recognized Ryder and seemed excited to see the "special guest," but everyone wanted to know where Deena was. She was the big draw. "Don't worry, she's on her way!" I assured them. Everyone cheered again.

The owner of the salon invited us into the back and offered us some drinks. That's when I got a call from Sid's assistant, with some perplexing news: they were still at the hookah lounge. "Andy, we've got a situation here. Deena's throwing a fit."

"What's the problem?"

"She didn't know about Ryder. She's pissed." It turns out that Sid never told Deena's rep that Ryder would be there.

Why was that a problem? Well, it seems that there was history between Deena and Ryder. From my understanding, Deena had

had a major crush on her Jersey co-star Pauly D., and she wasn't too pleased when Ryder put the moves on Pauly in the season opener and ultimately fucked him. For that and who knows what other reasons, she hated Ryder's guts, and didn't want to be anywhere near her.

"All right," I said, "so we'll keep them in separate rooms."

"No good. Deena wants to go home. She wants the limo to take her back to the airport right now."

That wasn't going to happen. Deena was the big attraction here, the mega-star, we needed her. "Send her limo over here, we'll work something out," I said. If worse came to worst we could put Ryder on the sidelines until the gig was over; she wouldn't be happy with that, but at least she'd get paid.

"No, Deena wants out. She says if we don't take her to the airport this second, she's going to call the police and claim that she's being kidnapped."

I stifled a laugh, and then did a quick calculation: would that be a good thing for us or a bad? "DEENA FROM JERSEY SHORE CLAIMS SHE WAS KIDNAPPED!" Photo spreads in the Post and the Enquirer, stories on TMZ and The Insider...Great publicity! On the other hand, police, lawyers, jail...Nah, not worth it.

"Where's Sid?"

"I don't know," said his minion.

Typical fucking Sid! Keeping everyone in the dark and then disappearing. I tried to call him. No answer. Then I got a call from one of his business partners. "Sid's having chest pains. He went to the hospital." Smart move, Sid.

Okay, I had to handle this debacle myself. I called the assistant back. "Keep Deena there, I'll come over and talk to her."

"We're already on the way to the airport."

What?! "Turn the limo around!"

"Uh...I don't think so." Clearly he was in the grip of diva terror. There was no going back.

Should I drive to the airport and head them off at the pass? Where WAS the airport? What the fuck...? This was a disaster. Deena was supposed to be with us the rest of the night. EVERY-THING was advertised as "Deena and a Special Guest." Who would give a shit about the Special Guest if there was no Deena?

I needed time to think. How was I going to spin this turd and make it come out smelling like a rose? I tried to think of a good excuse—Deena just got sick; Deena just dropped dead—nothing seemed potent enough to offset the possibility of mob violence.

I pulled Mario aside and explained the situation to him. Several minutes later, as we were trying to devise a game plan or an escape route, a cheer went up out front. A limo was pulling up to the tanning salon. "Deena's here!" they all shouted. I felt a sudden wave of relief, and then just as sudden a feeling of nausea in the pit of my stomach. "Wait a minute, I thought..."

Sure enough, I opened the limo door, and the back seat was empty. For some reason the limo driver showed up at the salon after he dropped Deena at the airport, I guess because it was still on his schedule.

That empty limo was the final straw, and the mood of milling restlessness morphed into outright hostility. The crowd was starting to turn ugly, and it wasn't that good-looking to begin with. I had to address the issue before they broke out the pitchforks.

"Excuse me," I said, facing the sea of gloomy faces, "we just heard from Deena, and unfortunately, she's had a family emergency, and had to go back to the airport." An angry rumble surged through the crowd, although the family-emergency bid for sympathy seemed to check their outrage somewhat. "We're really sorry—and so is Deena—but Ryder is here, and she'll answer your questions, sign autographs, whatever!"

Whatever the "whatever" was, it wasn't enough to satisfy the fans. They wanted Deena or they wanted blood! And even as I was scrambling to placate them, I had to wonder at the propensity for ordinary people to be obsessed with other ordinary people. Deena wasn't anyone they personally knew, and under normal circumstances you probably wouldn't cross the street to see her. But she was on Television, and that made her Significant. She was now worthy of worship and curiosity and criticism. Even by ridiculing her you were giving her more attention than made sense.

Anyway, all this put Ryder in a really awkward spot; she did her best to make it work, but the whole situation sucked. It got even worse as we moved on to the travel agency and the pizza place. Everyone was asking where Deena was, and getting pissed at us even though we had nothing to do with it.

The nightclub was the low point of the evening. The manager went ballistic on us. She was yelling and screaming and turning purple. "This is bullshit! I have a contract with Sid!"

"So take it up with Sid, then!"

"Okay, where IS he?"

"He's in the fucking hospital! Look," I said, "Ryder is here—she's honoring her contract—so don't bust our balls! We're doing the best we can!"

All true, but that didn't make the fans any happier. I felt so bad for Ryder—she was a real trouper, and she didn't deserve this. I considered her a friend and barely knew Deena.

Always the optimist while I am freaking out, my buddy Mario had an inspiration. He came to these events to do what he does best: drink alcohol and hook up with hot girls. A little setback like this—losing the main attraction and leaving 1000 angry Jersey Shore fans with a 'Special Guest' who they weren't that excited for—wasn't enough to stop him. So he got out his video camera, which he conveniently brought with him, and did an impromptu 'casting call.'

"Who wants to be on a reality show?" he shouted to the crowd. He started interviewing the nightclub customers on video, and promised them that we would use our "powerful connections" in the industry to send their audition tapes to reality production companies. Maybe one of them would be the next Snooki!

Personally I wasn't optimistic about that—even for non-talents the pool here looked pretty shallow—but it helped change the subject and got things moving in an upbeat direction. The fans started getting into it, playing up to the camera, and even the manager started to calm down a little. Before long there were hundreds of people in line to audition, we were all relaxing and having fun, the music was blasting, the drinks were flowing, and the groupies were willing.

But I had learned my lesson. No more pairing up with other reps without getting the full story in advance. The stress just wasn't worth it.

Talk about stress, and right away that brings me to another one of my clients from *The Jersey Shore*, who was actually a pretty big name. Everybody knew her.

Not everybody liked her.

Angelina.

Angelina and Mario in the limo on the way to an event

Angelina Pivarnick was far and away the show's least popular main star. Why this was the case, I'm not sure. True, she could be an overbearing egotistical pain in the ass, but not enough to make her stand out in a crowded field. There was just something about her that didn't really connect with the audience, and the harsh reality was that even huge fans of the show weren't huge fans of her. As a result, Angelina was only on for a couple of seasons, 1 and 2. She faded fast from the Jersey spotlight.

Because of this, she contracted for the least amount of money out of all of the *Jersey Shore* cast members. The Situation, Pauly D, and Snooki all commanded over $30,000 for a nightclub appearance. Angelina was lucky to get $2,000. Not that $2,000 is chump change, but it was on the extreme low end of the Jersey Shore pay scale.

Angelina found this grossly unfair. Why wasn't she getting whisked all over the world in private jets, like her former co-stars? Why wasn't she cashing big paychecks and getting the royal treatment?

Because she wasn't as popular, of course, but she never quite processed that fact. Feeling disrespected by the people who were hiring her, she would often shoot herself in the foot by acting the high-handed A-list diva. Her inferiority complex would sometimes kick into overdrive, often making her become demanding, whiny and obnoxious. I knew I was going to have my hands full whenever I booked her.

But business is business, and I was always jazzed when I could book an appearance near my hometown. So when a nightclub in Saratoga Springs, NY, only 30 minutes from my hometown of Albany, gave me a call asking for an affordable Jersey Shore star to make an appearance, I was excited. We talked over the list of cast members and their prices. Phil, the owner, was a little disappointed that Angelina was the only one within his price range.

"As much as I would love Pauly D at my club, that's just way too much money," Phil said. "Does he really get $30,000?"

"Oh yeah, definitely, at least, sometimes way more." I replied, "Demand for him is huge, so he gets the big bucks. But Angelina is still a great draw. Everybody knows her." And hates her, I neglected to add.

"Okay, let's go with it, then. Can I get her for August 21st?"

"Hmm, August 21st...hold on, let me check her schedule." Actually I couldn't check her schedule because she didn't have a schedule. I already knew she was available on August 21st, 22nd, the rest of August and the rest of the year for that matter. After a sufficient pause I got back to him. "Wow, looks like that's her only Saturday open. If you want it it's definitely yours. But we should lock it in now—it probably won't last."

After working out the deal with Phil, I texted the good news to Angelina: Saratoga Springs, August 21. I was pretty impressed with myself that I'd managed to book a gig for her, and I figured she'd be over the moon.

In her reply text, she wanted to know how much money she was getting, how she was getting to the gig, where she was staying, and what they would be giving her at the appearance (regarding type of alcohol, etc.). Was there a "thank you" buried in there somewhere? I couldn't find it. She must have forgotten it in all the excitement.

Of course, I lined up Mario to drive Angelina up from Staten Island. We would meet in Albany and then head up together to Saratoga. On the 20th he texted me that he would pick her up the next day at 3 pm. I sent the info on to Angelina, and she texted back, "Cool." That's what I wanted to hear. Cool. Everything's cool.

The next morning…

I was waiting patiently by the Keurig for my essential first cup of Green Mountain coffee when the phone started vibrating. It was my man Mario, checking in.

"Mario! What's up?" I asked as I picked up the cup from the machine and took a sip of the hot, smooth coffee.

The ensuing silence couldn't have lasted half a second, but I sensed in that briefest of hesitations the troubling promise of dark things to come.

"Don't be pissed at me, dude," Mario finally said.

See, that didn't sound good. "Why would I be pissed?" I asked, trying to sound unconcerned.

"I forgot, I promised my parents I'd go to some family reunion shit thing, and no way I can get out of it."

"So…?"

"So I can't drive Angelina tonight."

I choked on my coffee. "Are you fucking kidding me?" I said, trying to control my shock. "A family reunion? You're over 30 years old! You don't have to do everything your parents say."

"You know how they are. I promised them."

"What about what you promised me?!" I shouted back. I was starting to lose it. Mario rarely ever screwed me over, and I understood family commitments. But this I really, really didn't need.

"I'm sorry man, nothing I can do. Tell her to take the train up."

"Yeah, that's gonna go over well with easy-going Angelina," I thought as I hung up and tried to figure out a plan.

Okay, the problem was simple: Angelina was in NYC, and by tonight she needed to be in Saratoga. A flight was out of the question; too expensive, and the club wouldn't pay for it since it wasn't in the contract. A paid private car service would cost almost as much as a flight. The train, however, was not such a bad idea. It was cheap and easy: only $80 roundtrip from New York City to

Albany, and I could pick her up at the Albany train station myself and bring her to Saratoga. I started breathing a little easier. Yeah, a nice, relaxing train ride should work fine.

Good as the idea was, I still had to sell it to Angelina. My heart was beating fast, fueled by anxiety and caffeine, as I called her number.

"Angelina....?"

"Hey Andy," said Angelina brightly. "Don't worry, I'm set for tonight, I'll be ready at 3 pm. What's the guy's name—Mario?"

"Actually, there's been a change in plans," I began, carefully crafting how I would relay the news to her. "Mario's had a family emergency." (Just love the family emergency excuse.) "He's really upset that he can't drive you up tonight. He was really looking forward to it."

In true narcissistic fashion, Angelina didn't even ask what the family emergency was, which was good because I didn't have a back-story ready. Staying dutifully focused on herself, she took the news with a shrug. "So who's picking me up, then?"

Here we go, I thought, the moment of truth. Either she's going to be chill or she's going to flip out.

"Well, no one else is available on such short notice." I started cautiously, then followed it up with a burst of optimism. "So here's the plan: I'll reserve a train ticket for you from Penn Station, and I can pick you up at the Albany station myself!"

A moment of silence. Then—

"WHAT?!" Angelina screamed. "The TRAIN?"

"It's a great trip," I assured her. "I do it all the time."

"No way in HELL am I taking the train. Fuck THAT!"

Okay, she was showing an initial reluctance. Time to start talking faster. "No, the train is actually really comfortable, and it only takes 2 hours and 15 minutes from New York City. You can just sit back and stare at the Hudson River."

"I don't give a fuck about the Hudson River! No way! I'm not dealing with a public train and getting recognized. You know how many haters I have out there? I'd be putting my life at risk!"

This was actually an excellent point, but I chose to ignore it. "I think you're overreacting a little. Look, if it makes you feel better,

I'll get you an extra train ticket so you can bring a friend with you. Cool?"

"No, not cool!" she responded. "Hire me a car service!"

I gently explained to her how expensive car services are. It's funny, but some reality show stars are surprisingly clueless about actual reality.

Angelina was unmoved. "Well, you got me this stupid gig, you figure it out. I want a ride from my house or I'm not coming tonight!" And she hung up.

Gotta love the divas. Now I had to figure out an alternate plan or I was screwed in more ways than one. If Angelina didn't show up, we wouldn't get paid. More than that, it would be a breach of contract with the nightclub; they'd never want to work with me again—and why should they, if I couldn't deliver the goods? And if the word spread to other clubs that I was undependable— yeah, I was totally fucked. I tried to stay calm but I was quickly approaching freak-out status.

I walked outside to get some fresh air. It was late morning, and there wasn't a cloud in the sky. Families were walking together down the street, carefree, enjoying a weekend day with no respon- sibilities. Why couldn't I be one of them? Why I couldn't I just relax and enjoy a sunny, warm August afternoon? What was I doing in this stupid business?

Making money, that's right. Let's focus on the issue at hand. Should I just drive down to New York City myself, pick her up, and drive her back? No, that would be too crazy. There had to be another way. Maybe one of my friends from downstate would be willing to come up for the night and drive Angelina. I sat on the front steps outside, and made my first call.

"Hey Tom, what's up, it's Andy, how you been?" I said in my best casual not-looking-for-any-favors voice.

"Andy! Long time no talk. What's up?" said Tom.

"Hey, check this out—I have one of my reality stars from *The Jersey Shore* booked for an appearance in Saratoga tonight, but I have no way to get her up here. Any way you'd consider driving her? I'll make sure you get open bar all night. It'll be a fun time."

"Who is it?" he asked. "Snooki?"

I took a breath. "No—Angelina."

"Oh—ha haha. That would be hilarious."

Great—I had him hooked. "Okay, so let me give you the details…"

"Uh—hold on a minute."

Where was he going? I kept the phone to my ear, anxiously awaiting his return. If he said yes I could just relax and get excited about the night to come. If not…

Minutes went by and I was still on hold. What the hell was taking him so long?

"Andy." He was back on the line. "Sorry about that. I had to run it by the girlfriend." And…? "She says no, sorry, bro."

I couldn't believe it. "What, you need permission from your girlfriend to do anything now?"

"I just don't wanna piss her off. You know how it is."

"Not really, I'm single."

"I wonder why."

Touché, you bastard. "Thanks anyway, dude."

I had the same exact conversation with three more people. No. Nope. Sorry. No one was available.

Back to the laptop, and my last resort: Facebook. Surely one of my countless New York City-based Facebook friends would be interested in driving Angelina upstate for the night.

I posted on my profile: "Who's interested in driving Angelina, from MTV's Jersey Shore, from New York City up to Saratoga tonight? The perks—getting to hang out for a few hours on the drive with Angelina, VIP at her nightclub appearance all night, and open bar while you're there! Let me know ASAP."

I didn't have to wait long. Within seconds my "friends" were sending supportive comments.

"She sucks," one posted.

"Haha, you couldn't pay me to drive that bitch," said another.

"She isn't worth the free drinks."

The more polite among them were working, or too tired, or unavailable in one way or another.

But finally there came a promising post, from my friend Sarah: "Andy, call me, I might have an option for you."

I could envision the option already: Sarah lives in New York City but her parents are from Albany. I wasted no time making the call.

"So Andy, you need a ride for Angelina?" Sarah asked.

"Yeah, are you planning to come visit your family upstate tonight? That would work out perfectly."

"No, actually my parents are visiting me down here and they're driving home later. My sister Kristin's with them, and she's a huge *Jersey Shore* fan. They said they would drive Angelina up."

"Your parents?" I said, kind of dismayed. "I don't know if Angelina is gonna go for that."

"Do you have any other options?"

Did I? Not really. I needed to get Angelina up here, and this was my only shot. But how would the prima donna react when I told her that I had some family driving her? Probably not well.

I made the fateful call: "Okay, Angelina, I found you a ride. My friend's parents are in the city and they're heading upstate this evening. They would be happy to drive you."

"Your friend's parents?" she asked, as if not quite absorbing the information.

"They're really nice." I'd never met Sarah's parents, but I wasn't going to let her know that. Odds are they were probably nicer than Angelina, anyway.

"So like, an old couple?" she said.

"Yeah."

She was surprisingly unfazed. "Well, whatever. As long as they don't bother me. I'm gonna sleep the whole ride anyway."

That was probably best for everyone. "They're going to pick you up at 5 o'clock, so be ready."

"I'll be ready when I'm ready," she responded.

Damn, I thought to myself, why does she have to be so bitchy? But at least I had a ride for her and she was going to make it to the gig. All was right with the world. Now I could concentrate on important issues, like which of my old friends were gonna party with me tonight. It's always great when I'm doing a hometown gig—I can triple the size of the guest list and put a shitload of friends on it, and show them a good VIP time. It's fun to play the big shot once in a while.

And that put another idea in my head: a limo for the night would be great! I called a contact I have at the Picture Perfect Limo Company:

"Yo Jim, it's Andy. I have a *Jersey Shore* cast member in town tonight. Wanna hook us up with a limo?"

"Which cast member?" Jim asked.

"Angelina."

"Eh, I don't know. If it was Snooki then I'd hook you up in a second."

"It's Jersey Shore, man. We'll get a picture with her standing in front of your limo. And then you can advertise on your website that you drive Jersey Shore cast members around. Great publicity for you."

Jim liked the idea. He had an extra limo available, so he agreed to take our star from Albany to Saratoga and then back again after the event. "I'll comp it for you as long as I get the picture with Angelina."

Hell yeah! We were going to ride in style. Hopefully the limo would make Angelina happy and erase any residual annoyance about the drive up.

Psyched that everything was finally working out, I vegged for the rest of the day. It was just around 5, and I was getting ready to iron my party shirt for the exciting night ahead, when my phone started vibrating.

"Hi Andy, it's Kristin, Sarah's sister. So, um, we're at Angelina's house and um, she doesn't want to come."

"She doesn't want to come?!" I said, surprised and yet not surprised. "What's wrong?"

"Um, well, let me put her on the phone. . ."

A few seconds later.... "Andy!" Angelina snapped at me. "What the hell is this? You send some family to pick me up?"

Stay calm, I told myself. Work the problem. "I told you, my friend's parents would be driving you up, remember?"

"Yeah, but you didn't tell me someone else would be in the car too!"

"That's just my friend's sister. She's very nice..."

"But I'm bringing my friend! We're gonna be all crammed in the backseat! This is bullshit!"

"You didn't tell me you'd have a friend with you, Angelina," I said quite reasonably.

"I didn't think I had to tell you. Anyway, forget it, I'm not coming."

"Excuse me?" Here comes the stress again....!

"You heard me, I'm not doing the appearance. Fuck this."

A few seconds later Kristin got back on the phone, sounding on the verge of tears. "Andy, I'm so sorry, what do you want me to do?"

"Could you just ask your parents to sit tight for a few more minutes? Don't worry, it's gonna work out."

How was it gonna work out? I had no idea. My heart was racing again. I couldn't believe it—Deena and Ryder all over again! The whole night was going to be ruined, I wouldn't get my money, the club would blacklist me, my friends would be pissed off...Jesus Christ! A perfect fucking storm!

I took several deep breaths to try to calm myself. It didn't work. But there was no time to waste. I had to get Angelina into that car. I called her back.

I tried to get in the first word, but she was too fast for me. "I told you I'm not coming, Andy! You fucked up! Deal with it!"

"Angelina, listen," I said, amping up the desperation, "we have a contract with the nightclub. If you don't come it's a breach of contract. You don't want to get sued, do you?"

"I have a lawyer, I'm not worried."

"Okay, but you realize I won't be able to work with you again, ever, right?"

This gave her pause. Either that, or she was just confused. "What do you mean?"

"I mean, if a nightclub tries to book you, I'll have to tell them you aren't available, and recommend they work with someone else. You'll lose out on a shitload of money."

Silence. Good. I had her thinking. I knew she needed the money. And surely she could put up with a little inconvenience if her future earnings were in the balance. I was tempted to point this out to her, but I sensed that I shouldn't interrupt her brain when it was deep in self-absorbed calculation.

A few seconds later…"Fine, asshole. I'll go." I sighed with relief. "But don't ever pull this shit again! The backseat of some loser family's car…! Un-fucking-believable! "

"Hey, you're the one who wouldn't take the train."

"Fuck you, Andy. Tonight better be fun," she said. "I'm expecting a limo."

So much for my big surprise. This girl expected a limo as a matter of course. Sometimes I had to step back and marvel at the sheer mass of self-regard that propelled these Z-listers forward. Angelina was lucky to be making $2,000 cash to party at a nightclub for a few hours. But she expected more!

Ah, well—these were the devils I was dealing with.

I called back Kristin, and she told me everything was cool, they were in the car already and on their way. I knew we couldn't go into any more details because she was sitting in close quarters with the queen right now, so I kept it brief: "Great, thanks, and please thank your parents so much. I owe you."

"I know," she said.

Okay, it would be a few hours before Angelina arrived in town. I could try to relax, but what was the point? I was too anxious and wound up, so I headed over to the hotel to check in. I had worked out two complimentary hotel rooms in Albany for the night.

To my pleasant surprise there was a beautiful blonde working behind the hotel front desk. Time to put on my game face and drop some names. Nothing impresses these upstate people like the possibility of meeting a celebrity. Maybe I could coax some nice perks out of her: free room service, complimentary drinks, whatever.

"Hey," I said to her, "just checking in. I'm with Angelina Pivarnik—Angelina from Jersey Shore?—she's staying here tonight, and I want to make sure that everything's in order before she arrives."

"I hate that show," she said flatly. "You actually work for those people? What's wrong with you?"

So much for the perks. I grabbed the room keys and headed up to the hotel room to await the arrival of my "star." Lying on the bed, I let my mind drift as I thought about tonight, our exclusive

VIP room, the plush purple couches, the hot girls on either side of me, asking how they too could be reality TV stars... "It's easy, baby, easy..."

The dream started to take a really promising turn when all of a sudden my phone began to vibrate and I jerked awake. It was Kristin. Shit, now what?

"Andy? We're pulling up to the hotel."

Hallelujah! As I walked outside I heard a car door slam. Angelina and her friend were walking away from the car with their luggage, bitching to each other.

"Wow, that was hell," I heard Angelina say to her friend.

"I can't believe we had to just do that," agreed her friend.

Ignoring the two divas for a moment, I went up to Sarah's parents and Kristin. "Thanks so much for doing this. I'm so sorry about that whole business. These reality stars unfortunately have a mind of their own."

"Oh it's fine," Sarah's mom said cheerily. "Sarah prepped us. We were expecting a unique experience."

"Well, at least you have a story to tell," I joked.

"Yeah," Kristin chimed in. "Even though she was kinda rude, it's still pretty cool that I got to drive Angelina from New York City to Albany."

They were all such nice people. This was the real real world that you never got to see on TV. I felt so bad they had to deal with the unreasoning wrath of the Z-lister. As I turned back to the hotel, I saw Angelina and her friend over by the entrance, staring at me with the look of death.

"Where's my room key?" Angelina demanded. "We wanna get ready and have some drinks." Not even a hello, or an introduction to her snotty friend. Frankly, at this point I didn't really care.

"You're in room 648," I told her. "The limo will be here in an hour. Will you be ready in time?"

"Probably."

We got in the elevator, and despite her bitchiness I still apologized to Angelina for the hassle. Her gracious reply was, "Whatever. You can make up for it tonight." Angelina and her friend headed into their room, and I went back to my room to wait.

It was 10 pm when I heard a knock on the door: Jim, our limo guy, right on time. Miraculously, Angelina and her friend were actually ready. We all headed downstairs, got the money shot of Angelina in front of the limo, and hopped in.

As we cruised up the Northway to Saratoga, I sank into the soft interior of the limo, tipped my head back, closed my eyes, felt the tension seep out of me, and reflected on the craziness of the day. Somehow it had all worked out. Somehow sanity had prevailed.

Over the soothing purr of the limo engine, I heard a voice: "Sorry if I was a bitch today, Andy. I can't help it."

What? What did I just hear? I looked over in shock and saw Angelina smiling across at me, lit by the neon blue glow of the inside limo lights. I wasn't imagining it. Angelina was apologizing. To me. Holy shit.

Totally unprepared for this, I mustered up a jokey shrug. "I know you can't, Angelina," I said. "It's the Z-list curse."

"What do you mean?" she asked.

"Never mind," I said.

Angelina shrugged, and asked for a shot of vodka. I happily poured out three shots, and we all cheered to a fun night ahead.

Jim looked back at me from the rear view mirror as he drove the limo north to Saratoga. All he could see was a dude doing shots with two hot chicks, one of them a celebrity. I could read his eyes clearly: "You're a lucky guy, Andy, a lucky guy indeed."

True. Sometimes. But the luck seemed to be happening less and less.

CHAPTER 12
DOWNHILL

THEY SAY YOU NEVER HEAR THE bullet coming that knocks you off.

I guess you could make that case for *The Jersey Shore*. It truly hit so big and so fast that nobody was ready for it, and in no time at all it became the highest rated show in MTV's history. And if it was not for *The Real World* preparing the ground and creating the reality-show audience, *The Jersey Shore* probably never would have existed. Whether that's something to be proud of or apologize for is a matter of opinion.

But the downside was, once *Jersey* became such a massive hit, it sucked up all the oxygen in the room and left everyone else gasping—including *The Real World*. Suddenly there was a high demand for *Jersey Shore* cast members, and nobody else. Fewer and fewer venues wanted to book my *Real World* clients. It was all *Jersey Shore*, all the time.

This was not just a blow to my pride—there were real consequences to confront. As *Real World* cast prices started dropping, so did my commissions. Not only was I dealing with more and more Z-list ego bullshit and drama, I was getting paid less and less for it. Which made me wonder, was all this really worth it? Sure the perks were fun, but how many times can you drink for free and meet random hot girls before it starts to get tired? Seriously, once things began to slip I was nervous that it would all keep sliding downhill. If these Z-listers' fame and value were decreasing, and I was just an agent for them, what did that make me?

And I was torn. I had loyalty to my old clients, many who had become great friends, but their value was dropping dramatically, and I was practical enough to see the handwriting on the wall. The real money was with those superstar reality characters who were thrust into the spotlight by *The Jersey Shore* tidal wave: Snooki, Pauly D, Vinny, The Situation—they were making HUGE money. Up to $50,000 an appearance! Damn, if I could rep them, I'd be rolling in real dough.

Yeah, if. But no matter how hard I tried, I couldn't make it happen. Like I said before, the biggest Jersey names had signed up with high-powered reps right away, before I could even give them my pitch. Even Snooki, whom I had met long before *Jersey Shore*, signed with someone else, a guy her dad knew who ran an entertainment business. Don't get me wrong, Snooki's manager is awesome and I've done a lot of work with him throughout the years. But still, I was jealous that it wasn't me.

I kept trying to figure out how to gain the attention of the huge *Jersey Shore* stars. But I kept failing. I was literally experiencing failure after failure, which was not in the Binder tradition. Still, I wasn't going to give up just yet. I kept hustling, scooping up clients where I could and booking as many events as I could. And at least I had Angelina and Ryder; maybe they were *Jersey* leftovers, but still they were names attached to a huge show and recognized by almost everyone in the entire country. I was able to get them booked once in a while, and I was also booking some of the more famous *Real World* and *Challenge* cast members as much as possible. No, I would not be closing shop any time soon. The question was, could I satisfy the demands of the club owners and promoters, and provide enough "talent" to make it profitable for me?

I was sure as hell going to try. But circumstances being what they were, I knew I'd have to leave myself open to all options. So when my old nemesis Sid, whom I swore I would never work with again, called with a proposition, I was happy to listen. Sid, who seemed to have recovered nicely from his "hospital visit" in the Deena fiasco, now wanted me to bring together Angelina, Kenny, and Ryder for one night at a teen club. "Great idea!" I said, and I proceeded to squeeze as much money as I could out of him to make the deal.

Now sure, Sid was sketchy. Sure, he fucked us over last time. Sure, he booked us at random restaurants and stores before the main event each time, and pocketed the extra cash for himself. But money is money. And for all of the aggravation Sid caused, he was also well-connected in his city of Rochester, and always put us up in decent hotels, provided a limo, and brought us to top-of-the-line places to eat. So, all things being equal, I figured I might as well take the cash and hope for the best with this Triple Z-list appearance.

After being assured by Sid we won't have a repeat of last time, and after convincing Ryder we need the money and should give Sid one more chance, the deal was confirmed.

Kenny was going to fly into Rochester from out west, and Ryder was getting a ride with a friend of hers. Only Angelina, once again, needed a ride. I was not about to let the chaos, drama and stress from last time replay itself, so before I even called her to tell her about the gig and find out if she was available, I made sure Mario was in.

'I can do it," he assured me.

"Yeah, you say that now, but you can't back out at the last minute like last time. You have no idea the shit I had to go through with Angelina."

"Sorry about that. I won't let you down this time."

"Well, here's the deal: you pick up Angelina in Staten Island, then pick me up in Albany, then we'll drive out to Rochester. Can you handle that? Yes or no."

"Yes, I'm in! Gonna be awesome. *Jersey Shore* cast AND Kenny? Bobos everywhere!"

"This is a teen club event, you idiot. There won't be any bobos and there won't be any drinking."

"Okay—but how about afterwards, we can go out to the real bars, right?"

"Yeah, sure."

"Drinks and bobos!"

"Fine. Just no backing out, I'm counting on you for this ride!"

"No worries!"

Easy for him to say. Mario was usually reliable, but I was nervous after the last time. Plus he was getting more and more commitments with his real job, so I couldn't count on him to be our fake, alcohol-drinking, bobo-seeking, body-shot-pouring security guard driver as much as I used to.

Thankfully he kept his word this time. Mario got Angelina without incident, and they picked me up a few hours later in Albany.

"Got a coffee for you, Andy," Mario said as he handed me a Dunkin Donuts coffee, black with sugar. Just how I like it.

"Thanks man, appreciate it."

He handed me a straw.

"I don't need a straw with my coffee, dude," I said.

"It's perfect for hot coffee." He showed me his extra large coffee with a straw in it. "With the straw you can sip the cooler part on the bottom first," he exclaimed.

"That makes no sense, but to each his own," I responded.

Angelina opened up the passenger side door.

"Good to see you, Andy!" Angelina cheerily said, as she hopped out of the car. She got in the back and let me have the front seat.

I was surprised by her upbeat vibe. "Wow, you're in a much better mood than last time," I noted.

"Well, this was a much better ride than last time," she answered. "Mario showed up on time, he has a nice car, and he's funny as fuck. That's all I ask."

The sun was shining, and Angelina was in a good mood. It was a positive start to the day.

And we were making great time. Traffic was light and Mario was cruising west on the Thruway towards Rochester. All systems were go.

Until about ten minutes past Syracuse.

"SHIT!" Mario shouted.

"What?" I asked.

"I'm getting pulled over."

I looked back and saw the red siren lights flashing and coming up behind us fast.

"Sucks, dude," I said, knowing full well that sinking feeling. "But hey, there's worse things in life than getting a speeding ticket. Plus it's not like you were going that fast. Maybe they'll cut you a break."

He pulled the car over to the side of the road. "No, you don't understand," he said, his voice quavering in fear.

I didn't like the sound of this. "What don't I understand?"

Mario sighed heavily. "I got a DWI years ago that I never took care of. Never showed up in court and all that."

"WHAT?!" I exploded. "Are you serious? What the hell is wrong with you?"

"I forgot about it. It was back when I owned the pizza place in Albany. Once I sold it and moved to the city, I don't know, it just dropped my mind."

"It dropped your mind? How does a DWI arrest just drop your mind?"

"I'm a busy guy," he said in his defense. "I always made sure to drive carefully and not get pulled over. But there's probably a warrant for my arrest since I never showed up in court. So I'm fucked."

"You're fucked and we're fucked! If they arrest you we might not even be able to use your car!"

Mario was indignant. "That's all you're thinking about?"

"Look, I have to get Angelina to Rochester by 6, that's when Sid's meeting us. I have a contract to uphold."

"Sorry about your fucking contract, but I'm about to get fucking arrested. That's my focus right now."

Yeah, he had a point. The whole situation sucked. So much for our smooth, sunny, drama-free day.

"License and registration please," the cop said as he walked up to Mario's window.

"So sorry, officer. Didn't mean to be speeding," Mario said very calmly and professionally, trying to smooth-talk the officer. "If you can just give me a warning this time it would be sooo appreciated."

The cop responded positively to his overly polite manner. "You seem like a nice gentleman," he said. "You were only doing ten miles an hour over. I think this time I can let you off with a warning."

Relief poured over Mario's face. "Oh, that would be fantastic, officer."

"I'm just gonna go check your license real quick, then I'll be back and you can be on your way."

The grim dread came back over Mario's face. So close to avoiding the inevitable.

"FUCK FUCK FUCK," he said as he banged his fist on the steering wheel, while the cop got back into his car to look up Mario's information.

I felt bad for Mario, but I also felt bad that his idiocy had gotten us into this situation. And I was totally worried about getting to Rochester in time. In these shaky times I didn't need a hit on my reputation.

Angelina sat in the back, indifferent to the situation. She was a star, what did she care?

After what seemed like an eternity, the cop came back over to Mario's door.

"Step out of the vehicle, sir," the cop said sternly.

Mario unbuckled his seatbelt and got out.

I listened to their conversation on the side of the road through the open window.

"Put your hands behind your back, sir," the officer said to Mario.

Mario complied.

"Are you aware that you have an outstanding warrant for your arrest due to failure to show up in court for a DWI offense?" the officer said as he handcuffed Mario. "You're under arrest. You have the right to remain silent, anything you say or do can be used against you in a court of law...."

Mario interrupted, "I'm sorry, officer, honestly, I totally forgot. It happened years ago and I had a lot going on then and life took over and I'm just so so sorry."

"'Sorry won't cut it with this, sir. We're going to have to bring you into the station and tow your vehicle. Your friends will have to find another ride."

Shit, we were screwed. Find another ride where?

"Officer, if there's anything at all we can do to avoid that, please let me know," Mario pleaded. He went for the Hail Mary. "We have an event with Angelina from *The Jersey Shore* in Rochester tonight; she's in the car now. I just want to make sure she gets to her event in time."

There followed an ominous moment of silence. "Angelina from *Jersey Shore* is in your car?" the cop finally replied, in a quiet, even voice.

"Yes, I do security for all her events. Her agent is in the passenger seat, and she's in the back."

"Are you being serious right now?" said the cop, his voice rising a few decibels. "My wife and I watch *Jersey Shore* every week. We love that show. It's hilarious!"

Mario could see a lifeline dangling his way, and he grabbed for it. "Absolutely serious, sir—I wouldn't lie to an officer of the law." Then he had an inspiration. "I'd be happy to introduce you."

"Yeah, sure!" the officer exclaimed.

Mario walked over to the backseat of the car, still in handcuffs. "Angelina, could you get out for a minute?"

"Why?" said Angelina, clueless as to what was going on.

Mario kept his composure. "The officer wants to say hello."

Angelina sighed, and got out of the car. She walked over to the cop, and Mario made the introductions. The cop was ecstatic.

"Angelina! I can't believe this! My wife and I are huge fans!" He fumbled for his wallet. "Can I get an autograph?" he asked as he pulled out a dollar bill for her to sign.

"Ha, sure, no problem!" Angelina signed the bill and handed it back to him. "I doubt this will ever be worth more than a dollar," she joked.

"It will be to us! Can I get a picture with you too?" asked the cop.

"Of course. Mario, can you take our picture?"

"Umm—my hands are kind of restrained over here," he pointed out.

I could have jumped out of the car at this point to take the picture, but I was too busy marveling at the way this scene was playing out in front of me.

"Oh, sorry, let me take care of that!" the cop said as he went over and took Mario's handcuffs off.

Mario thanked him, rubbed his freed wrists, and then took several pictures of the officer and Angelina.

"Thanks again, Angelina," said the cop, pocketing his camera phone. "So great to meet you! My wife is gonna be so jealous she wasn't here."

"Great to meet you too, officer, have a wonderful afternoon," Angelina said, playing it real cool and professional, to my pleasant surprise.

As she got back into the car, the officer took Mario aside. Now we would find out if all this friendly hello-you're-wonderful bullshit was going to pay off.

"Okay listen," said the cop, "I shouldn't be doing this, but you have a celebrity with you and I understand you have to get her to an important event. I'm going to let you go, but you have to promise me you'll get this outstanding warrant taken care of as soon as you get back. Deal?"

"Deal! Thank you so much, officer. This means the world to me. Your sympathy and understanding are amazing. I'll never forget this," Mario said, kissing as much ass as possible.

They shook hands, and Mario got back in the car.

"Holy shit!" he exclaimed. "I can't believe it!"

"Yeah, Angelina just saved your ass!" I said.

"My smooth talking, too," he said.

"No, I'm pretty sure it was only Angelina." I turned to her in the backseat.

"Thanks for the help, Ang."

"No problem. Now let's get the fuck to Rochester already."

And with that Mario put the car into drive and slowly pulled off the shoulder, and we headed west to Rochester.

So for the second time now, the presence of a Z-lister had saved us from being carted off to jail. Chalk it up to the power of—what? Celebrity? Fame? But they were non-celebrities, faux-famous. I couldn't figure it out. And relieved as I was for Mario, and for the fact that we would make it to Rochester on time and it would all end happily ever after, I couldn't shake the gnawing feeling that it was all built on smoke and mirrors, that nothing could be less real than this world of reality. As we headed with symbolic aptness into the sunset, I was more skeptical than ever about where this career was taking me and in what direction I was going.

Mario, Ryder, Angelina, and Andy in the back room at the Rochester event

Sid was waiting for us at the hotel when we got to Rochester, and he handed me another dopey itinerary of on-the-way stop-offs. The tanning salon didn't want us back after the last disaster, but it looked like a grocery store was taking its place.

"How do you find these places?" I asked Sid.

"I'm a natural, what can I say?" Sid confidently responded.

"I'm glad to see you've fully recovered from your chest pains," I added sarcastically.

"Yeah, you're so funny, Andy."

Once Ryder and Kenny showed up, we all piled into Sid's limo to make the rounds of random stops before the teen nightclub event that night. They were all pretty ridiculous, with people lined up to meet the Z-listers at the grocery store, a strip mall, and a shitty restaurant. Finally the bullshit was over and it was time to return to the limo to get a ride back to the hotel and relax before the main event. But out of the corner of my eye I spotted a pile of flyers near the host stand at the restaurant as we were walking out. The flyer, with that day's date on it, had the following in bold letters on top:

"MTV'S JERSEY SHORE CAST PARTY TEEN NIGHTCLUB EVENT LIVE IN ROCHESTER, NY!"

Underneath, a picture of the *entire* Jersey Shore cast.
What the actual fuck?
"Sid!" I called over to him, as he was still trying to schmooze with the owner of the shitty restaurant. "What the hell is this?"
"What?" he said, annoyed that I was interrupting his rap.
"What the fuck is this flyer? The *CAST* of the Jersey Shore? You have ONE regular cast member here—Angelina. Ryder was only on a few episodes. And Kenny has never been on a Jersey Shore episode, ever. This is completely false advertising!"
Sid waved me off. "Chill Andy, it's fine. The kids will be happy that there are celebrities there, and then they'll get to party. It's all good."
"I don't think any kids will be happy if they're expecting the whole Jersey Shore cast, and basically NONE of them show up," I angrily responded.
Sid shrugged. "It is what it is," he said.
Yeah, right. "Good luck dealing with all of the lawsuits you'll probably get. And I'm telling you right now, we aren't walking into that club until you pay us the 50% you still owe us."
"Don't worry, you'll get it, relax."
I wasn't about to relax now, not with the shitstorm I could see looming just on the horizon. I showed the flyer to Mario, Kenny, Ryder and Angelina, and they were just as shocked as I was.
"Can he really do that?" Ryder asked.
"What the fuck am I doing here if this is a Jersey Shore cast party?" Kenny wondered.
Good point. His name wasn't even on the flyers. What the fuck

were any of us doing here? This event made absolutely no sense. I had just dealt with this kind of shit the last time I worked with Sid. I didn't think he'd do it to us again. I guess I was wrong.

We went back to the hotel and tried to mentally prepare ourselves for the debacle ahead. A few hours later we took the limo over to a huge event space that Sid had rented and transformed into a "teen nightclub" for the night. When we pulled up there were thousands of kids waiting in line to get in. It was winter, and the weather was freezing, and Sid hadn't opened the doors yet.

"Sid, they're standing out in the cold. Why don't you let them in?" I asked as the limo parked near the front door to draw attention.

"We wanted people to see the long line, and then the drama and the excitement of the celebrities pulling up in the limo. We'll let them in in a few."

"But they're freezing."

"Ahh, they're kids, they don't feel the cold."

Ridiculous.

Finally the line started moving, and I opened the door of the limo.

"Wait!" Sid yelled, annoyed.

"What?" I asked.

"Gotta wait until more of them are inside; then you guys can do a grand entrance and introduction on stage."

Should've known. Sid the master showman. But as we waited, I suddenly remembered, "Oh yeah, and you need to pay me. Cash please?"

"Yeah yeah, hold your horses, here you go," and he handed me the cash, acting annoyed again.

Why the hell should he be annoyed when he was the one putting us through all the bullshit?

Sid went inside, and the rest of us cooled our heels in the limo for at least another half hour. We were starting to get pissed, sitting in this limo in front of a falsely advertised event. The kids probably thought the whole cast of *Jersey Shore* was in here, and it only further convinced them when they tried to come over to the limo and Sid's fake bouncers blocked their paths.

Finally, Sid came back and told the limo to pull around back. We'd be going in the back entrance.

Really? We were sitting in front for almost 45 minutes to "get attention", and now he was bringing us in through the back? More vintage Sid bullshit.

We finally got into the building and were escorted through the back door to a tiny dressing room which at one point had been someone's office. We tried to stay in good spirits, as you can see in the picture of me, Mario, Ryder and Angelina hanging out in this tiny room waiting to be called on stage.

When Sid's security force finally escorted us over to the stage area, I could see that there were about 5,000 crazy teens in the hall. The place was filled to capacity. The DJ was blasting the hits, and these kids were dancing like there was no tomorrow, the excitement building for the arrival of the Jersey Shore "cast."

Then the DJ stopped the music. "Are you guys ready!?" he shouted into the mic.

Thousands of adolescent voices screamed louder than you could imagine. Sort of like how a One Direction concert would sound today.

The DJ continued: "Let me introduce to you a special guest we have in the house tonight! Star of MTV's *The Challenge*, host of *The Jersey Shore After Show*," (which was the only tenuous connection he had to the show) "and Jersey native, legendary reality star, Mr. Beautiful, Kenny Santucci!"

The teens looked surprised. An added celebrity they weren't even expecting. Awesome.

They screamed and cheered and went wild, as Kenny walked out on stage.

"What's up Rochester, so glad to be here! Let's party all night tonight!" Kenny shouted into the mic. More cheers.

The DJ continued.

"Okay, but that's not all! We have more! Please welcome to the stage, *Jersey Shore* 'star' and best friend of Nicole 'Snooki' Polizzi, Caitlin Ryder!"

Another "celebrity" the teens weren't expecting. They cheered again, screaming with excitement as Ryder took the stage.

"Hey, Rochester!" Ryder said into the mic. "Thanks for coming out tonight! We're ready to have a great time with all of you!"

More loud cheering.

The DJ went on.

"But that's STILL not all! Please welcome to the stage, STAR of MTV's *Jersey Shore*, the legendary, the loved, the amazing, Angelina Pvarnick!"

The crowd exploded! The first of the official *Jersey Shore* cast members taking the stage!

"Rochester my loves!" Angelina said as she grabbed the mic. "I hope you're ready to get wild and crazy with me tonight! Let's have a blast and dance all night! Give me a fist pump!"

And all the teens danced with the fist pump, a famous *Jersey Shore* cast dance move.

The DJ got back on the mic.

"Okay, let's get this party started!"

He blasted the music back on.

But nobody danced. The thousands of teens stood there in a baffled silence. And I could clearly read their expressions:

Where's the rest of the *Jersey Shore* cast? When are the big names coming out? This can't be all there is—can it?

A few minutes later—when they slowly realized that yes, it could, and that no more announcements and introductions of any more cast members would be made—the booing started.

And this wasn't just a few boos. All 5,000 teens were booing so loudly it was drowning out the music. So the DJ cranked the music louder to drown out the boos. But it wasn't working. We were about to have a riot on our hands.

"I told you," I said to Sid, who was standing near me.

"They'll get over it," he said.

"If this booing doesn't end in two minutes we're out of here," I told him.

"That would be a breach of contract."

I laughed. "I think you have more legal worries than we do, Sid."

The outrage continued for a few minutes, and then the teens seemed to realize that they could either keep booing the rest of the night or have fun with their friends. So they went back to dancing, and the crisis was averted. But every time I walked through the crowd I heard the complaints:

"I can't believe they lied to us," some guy said.

"We should sue whoever put this thing on," a girl said.

Maybe so, but it wouldn't be me or my team. We ended up staying the required time per our contract. If anyone would be getting sued over this debacle, it would be Sid, not us.

As soon as our three-hour commitment was up, we high-tailed it out of there and jumped into the limo, not even saying goodbye to Sid. If he needed a ride he could have one of his many "bouncers" drive him.

The limo dropped us off in downtown Rochester, and we went to the real bars for a few hours and ended up having a great time. The Z-listers were recognized, fans bought them drinks, and they in turn told the fans they should buy their agent and security guy drinks too. Which, I'm happy to report, they did. And Mario ended up getting to see some quality bobos.

So it all did end happily ever after, but the rest of the day was complete stress and bullshit. Was it worth it? Was dealing with pissed-off crowds who were lied to by the promoter worth the few hundred I was making for the night? This was the question I seemed to be dealing with after every event nowadays. Each gig seemed to come with drama, anxiety and stress. Either the Z-listers were giving me a hard time over some trivial bullshit, or the promoters were being cheapskates or sketch balls.

And those doubting voices in the back of my head were growing louder and more insistent. Why wasn't I making any progress in this business? I should be working with real celebrities by now. Why was I still stuck with Z-listers and making less money than I was a few years earlier? I couldn't get the big names, and my clients were losing ground. *Real World* was less popular, *Jersey Shore* was basically unreachable, and *The Challenge* cast was saturating the market.

And it just wasn't fun anymore. Even the partying was getting kind of old. Or maybe *I* was getting old. Either way, perhaps it was time to re-evaluate my life and my goals, and figure out where I wanted to go.

CHAPTER 13

THE LAST STRAW

STAGNATION. AGGRAVATION. FRUSTRATION.

It was all building to a crescendo. I knew it, I could feel it. Endless bullshit, endless drama. And for what?

Well, it was supposed to be for fun, and success, and money. But all those sources of enrichment were drying up, fast. And the temptation to give it all up seemed more than justified by the facts.

But I had invested so much of my time, my energy, and myself into this crazy business, and down deep I really truly loved it. So I tried to be optimistic, and held out hope for a little while longer. I knew there was still money to be made with the clients I had. And if I kept hustling away, maybe I could move up and out of the Z-list range entirely. Sure, the rollercoaster ride was coming to an end, but I didn't want to get off just yet. Maybe I could stay on for a second spin, and ride the car back up to the top. Why not?

There were about a hundred reasons why not, but I tried to

ignore them. The reality was, I was pegged as a Z-list agent, and there really wasn't any hint that that could ever change. But rather than acknowledge this, I kept grinding away, trying to get my *Real World*ers and *Challenge* stars booked wherever and whenever I could. Every day I was cold-calling, and sending out mass emails to nightclubs around the country. I would highlight the benefits of bringing in these reality stars, hyping them to the skies in the hopes that someone would bite. A sample, enticing e-mail:

MTV's Real World and Challenge cast members available for nightclub and bar appearances in your city! The cast members will MC/ host contests, do meet-and-greets and more! To help promote they will tag your venue on social media and do any radio call-in interviews you request. Plus, they're priced great, and guaranteed to bring in so many fans to your venue. Email me directly for specific pricing and availability.

I sounded like a used car salesman. Shit.

But that, in effect, was what I was selling, and sad to say nobody was buying. Until one afternoon, when suddenly it looked like all of these ridiculous mass emails would pay off in one fell swoop.

I received a response from one of the biggest nightclubs in Florida. They were interested in doing a weekly event with a reality star: a different star for each week, for the entire summer. Could I help them out?

Could I? This was essentially 10 gigs, confirmed in one e-mail! And the club even trusted me to pick which reality stars would be best, and lump it all into one contract. So in one single deal we were going well into the five digits on money coming in. It was a beautiful set-up, and if I played it right it absolutely had the potential to get renewed each summer and be a solid moneymaker in my back pocket for years to come.

It was a lot of work for me putting this puzzle together, figuring out which reality stars were free for which particular week throughout the summer. But I worked it out, and everything was finalized. The first week, the summer kick-off event, was going to be an appearance by Nehemiah Clark of *Real World: Austin*. He was on the original season with Wes, and they had remained great friends.

I knew Nehemiah well by this point, and was happy to book him.

I didn't plan to make the trips down to Florida each week—it wasn't paying well enough for that—but the club seemed professional so I figured all would proceed smoothly without my attendance. Such is my faith in human nature.

The night of the event I texted Nehemiah: *Everything going well down there?*

He replied a few minutes later. *The place is great! Thanks! Will text you if anything comes up.*

I reminded him of the most important part: don't forget to collect the money that was still owed to us. He said he was on it, and that was the end of it.

When I followed up with the club the next day, I asked the entertainment director, "How did it go?", crossing my fingers.

"Nehemiah was great to work with," he said. "Let's definitely bring him back again sometime soon."

"Sounds good to me, just let me know when!" I enthusiastically responded.

Nehemiah and Andy at an event

So Florida was off to a great start! And over the next few weeks, we had one successful gig after another. My stars showed up on time, did a professional job, and everybody was happy.

Could things be looking up? Would the drama and stress be over?

No.

A few weeks later, the scheduled gig was an appearance by Evan Starkman. Remember, Kenny's other half. He was there for Mardi Gras in 2009, our best year ever. I had worked with him for years. Trusted him. He was a friend.

Not this week.

I called him the night before the gig. "Hey man, you never sent me your flight info for when you get to Florida tomorrow. Can you send it over to me so I can get it to the club and they'll have someone pick you up from the airport?" I asked.

"Didn't get a flight. Can't do the gig," he responded.

Oh shit.

"What do you mean, you're can't do the gig?"

"I can't do it, man," he repeated.

"We have a contract!"

"I didn't sign it."

"The club did, and you verbally agreed to it! And you also accepted the terms over email. That's a contract!"

"Well, something came up, I just can't do it, sorry. Get someone else."

"Someone else? It's fucking tomorrow!"

"You have a lot of clients, you must have somebody."

See, the reality market was so saturated at this point that even the reality stars themselves figured they were a dime a dozen, anybody else could replace them and nobody would know the difference. Which was probably true in many cases.

But the club had promoted Evan. They wanted *him*.

"Not how it works, Evan. I need *you* there."

"Oh well, sorry man, but don't put this on me. You know I never personally signed the contract. This isn't my fault. I can't help you out this time." He hung up.

FUCK!

Really? Again? Drama? Stress? Could I not go just one month without dealing with some kind of bullshit at one of these appearances?

No time for self-pity. I had to think of an excuse fast.

I texted the entertainment director at the club and used my go-to excuse: family emergency, sorry, Evan has to postpone.

This was not received well. The director let me know that the club was upset; in fact, it was pissed. They had invested time and money in this event, and for us to back out at the last minute was unacceptable.

Looked like this guy wasn't going to let me off the hook so easily. I hurriedly texted back, *We feel terrible about this situation, but we'll be happy to reschedule Evan at your convenience.*

All good? No.

The director basically said to forget about rescheduling Evan. He also basically said it was clear I couldn't deliver on the promises I made in the contract.

I felt like shit. Even though it wasn't fully my fault, it was still my responsibility. I had vouched for Evan, and now my word had proven worthless.

There was nothing I could do at this point but move forward. And at least the next few weeks after the Evan cancellation went off without a hitch. But during that entire time I rarely had a positive thought about my career and what I was doing in the Z-list world. Everything I had feared about my tenuous grip on a once-successful business was coming to life before my eyes. It was all falling apart, and I couldn't do a thing to stop it.

To make matters worse, I received a letter in the mail from the club, threatening to sue me because I didn't honor the full contract terms.

I called the club. "I just got a letter from your lawyers. What's all this talk about lawsuits? I told you we'd reschedule Evan."

"We don't want to reschedule."

"So you're gonna sue me instead?"

"Consider this putting you on notice. If there's any breach of contract again we will go hard against you."

"What breach? There's a clause in the contract about sickness and rescheduling."

"You didn't provide any proof of sickness."

He was right, I didn't provide any, because I didn't have any.

"What can I do to make this whole thing right?" I asked.

"Not much. Let's just get through the last few weeks of our summer gigs. But," he added, "we probably don't want to work with you again."

Great. From a yearly summer bonanza to permanent exile in Siberia.

Could things get any worse?

Actually, yes. A few days later I checked out the club's website to see how vigorously they were promoting the last few weeks of summer events that we had booked there. I suspected they might downplay the shows because they didn't foresee us as future collaborators and saw no reason to give us unnecessary publicity. But no, we were still prominent on the schedule. At least the club wasn't going to cut off its nose to spite its face.

But as I went down the schedule, something unsettling caught my eye. There was an additional gig added.

It was Nehemiah Clark. Again. He was coming in the week after the last gig of the lump contract that I had with the club.

Needless to say, I didn't book that date.

I gave Nehemiah a call. "Dude, what's up with you going back to the Florida club?"

"They called me and asked me to do it. I figured you knew about it," he said.

"I didn't."

"Sorry man, you can take over the contract details if you want." Nehemiah was a classy guy, he respected the agent/client boundaries, and I appreciated that.

"Nah, just do what you're doing. The club is pissed at me anyway. That's why they went around me. Keep making your cash. Good luck, man."

I hung up and that was that.

But I had to recognize now that the rules of engagement had just changed overnight, there had been a shift in the plate tectonics, and nothing would ever be the same. Basically, there was no need for an agent anymore. The clubs could call or message the cast members and book them directly. The reality stars were so easily accessible on social media, why let an agent get in the way and drive the price up?

But hey, maybe my clients would fight to preserve their relationship with me. Maybe they would remember all the hard work I did on their behalf, hold the line and say "All for one and one for all!"

Nope. As I said, the problem was a saturated market: there were too many reality stars fighting for too few slots, and something had to give. The lowest-level Z-listers were desperate for work, and they wouldn't risk losing a potential payday by telling the promoter or club owner to call their agent. No, they took the gig on the spot. No need for reality-star agent extraordinaire Andy anymore.

Yes, I had become that most dreaded of things in show business: unnecessary and irrelevant.

Not only did my big club deal fizzle out, but so did many other deals. The bitter irony was, for years I was trying to leave the Z-listers, and in the end they left me. Only some of my bigger name clients kept their loyalty to me. Wes Bergmann, for instance, would only do an event that was contracted by me.

He trusted me. We were friends.

That wasn't true for many of the others. For them, my usefulness had run its course. Even when I did try to broker a deal, it would go something like this: I'd call up a club, they'd show interest, I'd quote them a price, and then they'd contact the reality star directly, and he or she would quote a lower price. I'd be cut out of the deal. End of story.

So what was the point of even trying? It was a waste of time. No deals, for no money.

Yeah, it was a dark time in the Binder world. After almost ten years on this wild ride, it was finally time to close up shop and find something else to do with my life.

CHAPTER 14

JUST WHEN I THINK I'M OUT. . .

HAVING MADE THE MOMENTOUS DECISION TO move on and not look back, to jettison this endless merry-go-round of drama and excess and Z-list egomania and follow my own destiny, I was now left to ponder a new question: What the hell *was* my destiny? What was I going to do next?

I didn't know. I knew I was completely fed up with the reality-star booking business: the cast members were getting ruder, the gigs were getting fewer, and the commissions were getting lower. Even the endless partying with Z-list groupies was getting tired. The payout in money and perks just wasn't worth the endless stress anymore.

But having turned my back on that miasma, what was I now qualified for? What did I have to offer? Over the years I had developed a very specialized set of skills: I knew how to handle over-sized egos and market them to a TV-obsessed public. How did those skills translate from the reality world to the real world?

As I evaluated my prospects, it became clear that there weren't a lot of great options. All my business contacts were in the circle of hell I was trying to escape from. And a lot of those people had left for greener pastures as well. Mario had long ago sold his pizza joint and moved on to construction management, so I couldn't even go back there and practice Smitty's Law.

With nothing concrete in the future, I nevertheless began the tedious process of gathering the paperwork to close up Tobinder Talent Booking, LLC. I fulfilled my final contracts, transferred money out of the business bank account and closed it up, and prepared to shut down the website. And through the whole process it was brought home to me even more forcefully how plain sick of it all I was. Even now, just thinking about how annoyed I was, it pisses me off. I was so over the Z-list world. It was done. Finito. So long, farewell.

And that's when I got the phone call.

Just like magic, like clockwork, like the past good luck which I thought was long gone—that very same week, my phone rang with an unrecognizable number. It was a Las Vegas area code.

Who did I know in Las Vegas? Who did I *want* to know in Las Vegas? Should I pick this up or save myself a lot of grief? Oh well…

"Yeah?"

"Can I speak to Andy please?" a higher-pitched male voice said.

"This is Andy—who is this?"

"Hey man, this is Jeff Timmons of 98 Degrees."

WHO? THE Jeff Timmons from the hit boy band 98 Degrees? Hey, I was used to talking to some pretty big names, but usually I was the one calling them. What could Jeff Timmons possibly want with me?

"I just found your website while I was doing a search online for agents," he went on. "I see you've done a lot of stuff with the reality star world. I'm wondering if we can set up a time to talk about possibly working together on some projects I have going."

I had to pause to process this unlikely information. Could this really be Jeff Timmons? The guy who co-founded 98 Degrees, the Grammy-nominated, multi-platinum-selling boy band? Timmons was famously responsible for bringing all four original members of the group—Nick Lachey, Drew Lachey, Justin Jeffre, and himself—together and helping to get them signed. Not only was he a celebrated singer, but he understood the entertainment business world inside-out and was responsible for all of his own successes.

And now Jeff Timmons, an established celebrity with actual talent, wanted to work with me? Shit!

I was stunned, but I hid my amazement behind my practiced casual, professional phone demeanor. "Mr. Timmons, thanks so much for the call. I would love to discuss working together."

"Andy, call me Jeff."

"Jeff."

"I see you have a 518 area code. Where are you from?"

"Albany, New York."

"That's what I thought. Great coincidence: I'm on tour right now and we have a date in Albany next week. We should meet up."

Yes, we should absolutely meet up! All the reservations I had about this pain-in-the-ass business were swept away in a millisecond. Meeting with Jeff Timmons? Pencil me in!

The tour he was speaking of was the 98 Degrees Reunion Tour. Called "The Package Tour", it also featured New Kids on the Block and Boyz II Men. They were selling out arenas around the country. I had already heard they were going to be at the Times Union Center in Albany the following week.

"Sure, I can come down to the arena and we can link up before or after the show, if that works for you," I said, struggling to conceal my enthusiasm.

"Sounds like a plan. I'll leave tickets and passes for you at Will Call. Just text me when you're there and we can figure out the plan," Jeff said.

For the next week I was suspended in limbo. My Z-list world was crumbling, I was hanging on by a thread. Had my lifeline just arrived? I wasn't sure yet, but I decided to hold off officially closing out the business and shutting down the website for just a few more days.

Actually the week went by pretty fast. I tried not to think about the meeting too much. I didn't know what Jeff had in mind, so no point in pondering whether this would be my resurrection or just the final nail in the coffin. I kept myself busy just doing my own thing, but in the back of my mind I knew that whatever happened at this meeting could possibly determine my entire future. For better or for worse.

No pressure.

On concert day, I went down to the arena with my friend, a girl who was obsessed with 98 Degrees when we were younger. We maneuvered around the thousands of fans flocking inside, I gave my ID to the person at the Will Call window, and within seconds she handed me tickets and meet-and-greet passes. They were labeled "JT", to note that Jeff Timmons had put my name on the list. It's good to be friends with the king.

The meet-and-greet came before the concert, so we went backstage and waited in line for a picture with 98 Degrees. I have to admit I felt kind of awkward back there. There were about thirty people in the meet-and-greet. All females, early 20s to 40s. And me. I wasn't complaining, but still, it felt kind of weird waiting in line with all of these hot ladies to meet a boy band.

When it came our turn I snapped a photo of my friend with the group first, and then I went right over to Jeff. Jeff was 40 years old, but didn't look a day over 28. Muscular, tan, full head of brown hair. I was jealous.

"Hey Jeff, it's Andy Binder," I said, shaking his hand.

"Andy! Great to meet you in person!" Jeff said. He looked down at my excessive, stand-out, black and grey plaid Guess brand button-down shirt with sparkly beads on it. I wanted to look like a celebrity, what can I say?

"Nice shirt," he complimented.

"Thanks!"

Andy with the guys of 98 Degrees

I took a picture with all the guys, and then Jeff patted me on the back. "So how about I text you after our set, and we can meet up in my bus?" he suggested.

That was fine with me. My friend and I went out into the arena to find our seats. It turned out Jeff had put us in the second row of the VIP seating, right by the stage. Nice!

After Boyz II Men did their set, it was time for 98 Degrees. The lights dimmed, and pictures of each member of the group flashed on the screens by the stage. The crowd screamed in excitement.

How cool was this?—14,000 fans going nuts for this group, and I was meeting with one of its members after the show.

Amazing.

98 Degrees sang hit after hit after hit. These guys had so many memorable songs from back in the day. And the crowd was loving every one.

They finished up their energizing set, and left the audience completely exhilarated. After a 30-minute set change, New Kids on the Block came on, and the crowd erupted again. I thought some of my Z-listers got a good response, but this was the big leagues now, and there was no comparison.

About three songs into their set I got a text from Jeff:

Jeff: *Hey Andy, I just showered. Want to come meet me back by the bus?*

Me: *Coming now. I know where the buses are, I'll look for you out there.*

My friend was fine with staying and watching the show by herself. She knew I had business to take care of.

I flashed my pass to security and walked out to where the buses were. I found Jeff a few minutes later in between a few of the nicest tour buses in the pack.

"Hey man, thanks again for coming to meet up," he said.

"Oh, my pleasure, man!"

"Let's go in the bus and talk.' As he headed into the bus, he stopped to mention, "Just letting you know, I'm traveling with my family. I decided to get my own bus and bring them along on tour. The other guys in the group are on a separate bus."

Yep, he had his own multi-million-dollar tour bus. And if you've never been on a celebrity tour bus before, it is pure luxury. High end leather couches, beds, huge flat screen TVs, top-of-the-line sound system, kitchen loaded with food and drinks, elegant mood lighting, and the scent of burning incense. It was like walking into a Sultan's suite. Damn, did I want to work with this guy!

Jeff introduced me to his wife Amanda: a gorgeous blonde, in her mid-30s, who didn't look a day over 25. Also on the bus was their teenage daughter and her friend, as well as their school age son and their 2 year old daughter. They made a cute, very friendly family.

The introductions out of the way, Jeff sat me down in the "living room" of the bus and starting talking shop. "So basically here's what we have going on. My business partner and I have started a male revue called Men of the Strip."

"Men of the Strip...?" It was at that moment that I glanced over and noticed a stripper pole in the corner of the living room. Is this where they held auditions, I wondered? I looked over at Jeff's very wholesome family, scrolling on their iPads and playing video games, and then gave a confused look to Jeff.

Jeff laughed. "This was T-Pain's tour bus before we starting using it," he explained.

"Oh!" I said. "Makes more sense now."

"Anyway," continued Jeff, "Men of the Strip. The basic concept is based on the Vegas strip. Think Chippendales, Magic Mike, Thunder From Down Under. Only better. I host the show, and sing some of our 98 Degrees hits. Then the male dancers do a full performance, and they even sing too. Plus, of course, they strip."

`"Sounds great." I wasn't into male strippers myself, but I could see right away the kind of draw this could be. Music, dancing, sex. A can't-miss combination.

"Our goal right now is to get the brand out there. Build a fan base. We're looking to do clubs and small theaters to start. We'll be doing press in every city to help build the brand."

I nodded, still wondering where I fit in.

"I see you've done a lot of stuff with reality stars around the country," said Jeff, "which probably takes a lot of hustle."

He had no idea how much.

"And I'm guessing," he continued, "that you have some great

venue and promoter contacts. Would you be interested in helping us put a tour together, and booking some dates for us?"

Would I? Was Jeff Timmons really asking me to book a tour for him? Was this real life? I knew male revues were in demand now, and were generally profitable. But a male revue hosted by a member of one of the most famous boy bands in history?—this had big money written all over it.

"Absolutely!" I replied, balancing my professionalism with a hard-to-contain enthusiasm. I didn't want to sound over-eager, but shit, I wanted him to know I was in. "Just send me any promo material you have, and I'll get to work!" Jeff was delighted. "I think we can do a lot of stuff together, Andy."

I sure as hell hoped so.

To that end, I skipped the rest of the New Kids set, choosing to hang out with Jeff some more. We got to know each other better, and he seemed really pleased with the way this was panning out. "You definitely seem motivated, Andy. I'm looking forward to making this work with you."

So was I.

When the show ended, he let my friend come on the bus and get some personal pictures with him. She loved it.

I got to know Jeff's wife Amanda as well. She took a sisterly interest in my love life, and told me that when we started doing some Jeff and Men of the Strip dates together, she would make it her mission to find me a girl.

I liked her already.

After about an hour or two we said our goodbyes. They had to roll on to their next tour stop in Buffalo, and I had to get some rest. Tomorrow was the beginning of a new adventure!

It was a galvanizing night for me. The missing spark that first came to me when I met Veronica and Rachel a good decade earlier was back and burning bright. To think I'd been so close to giving up on it all just a few days before. Life had a funny way of working out sometimes.

And speaking of work... I spent the next few weeks calling every venue and promoter I had worked with in the past. I cold-called and cold-emailed hundreds more. And it paid off almost immediately. Within days I had my first offer. I texted the info to Jeff, and he confirmed it with me on the spot.

Great work! he said in his text. *Keep them coming.*

And I did. I was booking dates for thousands and thousands of dollars, and before I knew it we had a 35-city tour set up!

JEFF TIMMONS OF 98 DEGREES PRESENTS MEN OF THE STRIP!

That's how the show was officially billed in every contract.

And before I knew it I was listed as the main contact on the Men of the Strip webpage. Even beyond that, I was soon the main contact on Jeff's own webpage. Shit!

It was so exciting. All the hard work with the Z-listers was finally paying off. Over ten years of reality star experiences had prepared me for this next step that I was beginning to think would never come. And suddenly here it was: I was working with real talent, and had booked a full nationwide tour, that even included some stops in Canada. New venues and new opportunities were coming every day!

A month later the tour began, and it got off to a great start. Jeff had only amazing things to say. He raved about the way I put together the schedule. To tell the truth, I was pretty proud of my work too. But it was a few weeks into it before I got my first chance to finally go see Jeff and The Men of the Strip perform live. It was a club date at a huge nightclub in Toronto.

Of course, Mario wanted to come.

"A boy band member, and male dancers? You know what that means, right?" Somehow I *did* know. "Endless bobos!" he said.

"Dude, we're not doing Z-list anymore. You gotta be professional. If you can't be, then you can't come," I said.

He promised he would be on his best behavior, for the show, anyway. So he joined me for the six-hour drive to Toronto.

When we got to the club, we went backstage to say hi to Jeff. I introduced him to Mario, and he introduced us to his business partner Mike and the male dancers. Everyone was thankful and appreciative of all I had done to make the tour happen. They were excited, I was excited, and the vibe was amazing.

Mario even kept his promise—for about the first half hour that we were there. Then, as I was chatting it up with the guys in the dressing room, I looked over to see Mario making out with a random gorgeous girl he had met in the club. I couldn't believe he brought her into the dressing room! As I was about the go yell at him, the guys just laughed and waved me off. They thought he was hysterical, thankfully. But I was still annoyed at Mario for making that kind of first impression.

Then Jeff pulled me aside. He had a sort of sober look on his face. Uh-oh. What was this? Did something go wrong? Was he going to yell at me about Mario's unprofessionalism? Was he giving me the hook so soon?

"So Andy," he began, "You probably know I pitched this Men of the Strip idea to several agents. And you're the only one who really got it, and came through for us. You did an amazing job, and I want you to keep working with us and keep booking us."

Whew! Well, that worked for me. My commissions off these guys were huge, and Jeff was easier to work with than almost all my reality star clients. Why wouldn't I keep working with them?

"But there's been a new wrinkle," he continued. Shit. He wants me to share the work with a bigger name agent. He's putting me to the side, in a secondary role. Something like that, right?

"...And I wanted to be the first to tell you. We just signed a deal with a production company to film a two-hour docu-movie about us for the E! Network!"

Once again I needed a little time to process this. "E! Network? Are you serious?" I excitedly asked.

"Yeah man, they're going to film the end of the Men of the Strip tour, then shoot us in Vegas as we audition new dancers and try to find a residency on the Vegas strip. This is going to make us even bigger."

"Awesome! Congrats!"

"And you're going to be the guy booking the shows for us."

I was ready. Ten years ago I wouldn't have been. But the Z-listers had fully prepared me for this moment.

The Toronto show was a hoot to watch. The place was filled to capacity with screaming ladies, and they had plenty to scream for. The show was insane. Jeff and the guys delivered the goods in spades. Everyone was happy. Positive energy abounded.

A few months later the Men of the Strip two hour docu-movie premiered on E!. Within hours my phone was ringing off the hook. Call after call after call. Major casinos and huge theaters around the country wanted to book Jeff Timmons of 98 Degrees and Men of the Strip.

And I was able to negotiate higher and higher guarantees. $10,000 dates became $30,000 dates, which became $60,000 dates. My commissions were getting huge. And we were doing shows everywhere you could imagine, from Minnesota to Kansas to Halifax to, yes, that sold-out theater in Boston.

And every time I went to a show that I booked, I was drawn back to how I felt way back at the start—that original Matchbox Twenty concert at Geneseo, when I saw my 3,000 fellow students having the time of their lives in my college gymnasium. And knowing that I had helped make it happen.

And now it had really come full circle for me. I was responsible for making these huge shows happen. If I hadn't made the call, negotiated the contract and worked out the agreement between venue/promoter and artists, the show wouldn't be there. Those thousands of screaming happy ladies were enjoying themselves at the Jeff Timmons and Men of the Strip shows thanks to my hard work. It was a beautiful feeling, and I guess it was the reason I got into this business in the first place. Sure, I loved the money. I loved the ladies. I loved the partying. But most of all, I loved knowing that my hard work had helped make the worries of thousands of people go away for at least one night, and given them one of the best memories they would have for a long time to come.

That's what really made it all worth it.

CHAPTER 15

ONWARD AND UPWARD

MY STORY NEARS ITS END, BUT it wouldn't be complete without a nod to Johnny Bananas.

Things were rocking for me now. Men of the Strip had really taken off. In no time at all, they'd secured a home in Vegas at the Hard Rock Live. And who was in charge of booking their off nights from Vegas at venues around the country? That's right, I was (and still am).

Also, Jeff Timmons went back on the road with 98 Degrees, and he asked me to book him for after-party appearances during the tour, and solo concerts on his off dates.

It was a whirlwind. Representing real talent was incredible. It was what I was born to do. The shows were huge, the money was big, and the dates were plenty. And now I was in a position to increase my roster and represent more A-list talent.

But I still had a soft spot for my Z-listers. Hell, I never would have gotten anywhere if it wasn't for the reality TV world. Sure, that world had its crazy ups and downs, but it would always be a part of me. And even with my agency and bookings on the rise, I wasn't going to forget some of the reality stars who were loyal to me throughout the years, and who remained great friends.

Wes Bergmann, for instance—my good friend, and Area Code Girl Rating System creator. Wes always stuck by me, and never did an event without sending the inquiry my way. I respected that, and I respected him. I still do. He's one of the smartest guys I know.

Wes had been appearing on almost every season of *The Challenge* so demand for him was still high, and the increased access I now had to bigger clubs and venues only helped me get him more gigs around the country. I started booking him for bigger appearances and more money than ever before.

So I went back out on tour with Wes and we did some amazing gigs, had some great times, good memories (and a fight here or there for good measure), and brought in some big dollars—from a high end nightclub in Canada, to a wild college bar in Upstate NY, to an insane beach party in Rhode Island. Wes was a much tamer person this time around—he was engaged to the new love of his life, and his great boyfriend habits from when he was with Johanna still rang true. Oh, he'd still drink with me and try to hook my single ass up, but when the gig was over he was more than happy to head back to the hotel and go right to sleep.

Andy and Johnny Bananas in a limo
headed to the hotel before a gig

It's tough to get old.

All of this new-found success—the huge gigs with Jeff and Men of the Strip, the new bigger appearances with Wes—helped me gain the attention of some long-established reality stars. Most notably, the aforementioned MTV legend, Johnny Bananas.

Johnny had appeared on more reality shows than any other star in MTV's history. He was also the winningest cast member of *The Challenge*, with more cash prizes earned than any other star who has ever been on the show. I had met Johnny about a dozen years earlier when I first started out, and did a few gigs with him. But he had another agent he liked to work with, and he and Wes never really got along well, and my loyalty was to Wes. Their famous feud still plays out on all of the seasons of the *The Challenge* that they appear on together.

Now that we were older and presumably a little more mature, it was possible for me to represent them both. And when Johnny saw what I was able to do for Wes after all these years, he wanted a piece of that action.

I was hanging out at a reality-star hot spot bar in Manhattan when Johnny spotted me from a few tables away.

"Hey Winder Binder!" he shouted over to me. Johnny and Kenny Santucci were best friends, and if you remember, that's what Kenny liked to call me. So now Johnny did the same.

"Johnny, what's up man? How you been?" I asked as I walked up to him. All the girls in the bar were staring over in our direction. No doubt they had noticed the famous Johnny Bananas. I doubt they were mesmerized by me.

"Good, dude, thanks. I see you're doing well too. Booking all these tours and finding work for that ginger Wes," he joked, always coming up with ways to make fun of Wes, most notably his trademark red hair. "Shit, if you can get him all of those gigs, you should be able to get me even more, for more money. I'm more famous than he is."

"I'd say you're equally famous," I responded.

"Bullshit!" he said while cracking a smile.

I enjoyed breaking balls with Johnny, but I could sense he was angling for something more, so I bit. "Don't you have someone who handles your bookings?" I asked him.

"Not anymore. I couldn't trust him. I'll make you my main guy if you wanna do it."

That's what I wanted to hear. "So you're saying I can book and handle all of your events and appearances for you?" I asked.

"Yeah, I'll forward you all the inquiries from my website. I'm at Realjohnnybananas.com."

"I like how you still brand yourself."

"It's all about branding. You know that."

I did. And I liked the way Johnny thought. I told him to send me whatever he had and I would get busy locking in dates.

"Will do. Look forward to doing business with you, Winder Binder!"

It was a gratifying moment. Gone were the days of cold calls and cold e-mails. My business was getting name recognition now, and reality stars like Johnny Bananas were so huge that I didn't have to sweat like a used-car salesman to sell them.

The next day Johnny forwarded me about twenty e-mail inquiries from his website that he'd been too busy being Johnny Bananas to answer. I responded to all of them and booked several big money dates. I followed up with several of my own promoter and venue connections, and the moment I said I was representing MTV legend Johnny Bananas, they were all down!—and for much bigger money than I was getting for the lesser-known reality stars saturating the market.

And as it happened, the tour I booked for Johnny was one for the record books. It was, by far, the biggest reality star tour I had ever booked.

However, as experience taught me, everything couldn't be perfect. There were bound to be ups and downs with reality star events. Even (or especially) if the star was the legendary Johnny Bananas.

So let me indulge you one last time with an insider's look behind the scenes of a reality star tour. The Johnny Bananas Summer Tour featured stops at the following venues:

A really fun bar/nightclub in Hartford, CT, another wild club in Worcester, MA, a day party at a lakeside bar in Upstate NY, a sketchy concert venue in Queens, a beach party in Rhode Island (where I had already brought Wes), a hosting event at the largest nightclub in Atlantic City, and a private graduation party appearance.

Being the full service celebrity representative that I am, I not only booked and organized the whole tour for Johnny, but I also cleared my schedule so I could be with him the entire time. Driving him from city to city would be way easier than having him rent a car himself. Plus, maybe I was a little older now, but I still loved this stuff. Especially when I was working with celebrities who weren't going to screw me over.

The tour started with the graduation party. A very wealthy family was having a high school graduation party for their daughter, and they wanted it to be the biggest and best ever. Several of the graduates were fans of Johnny, so they were eager to book him for an appearance.

Private parties pay more than regular club events, and this one we couldn't turn down. The location was actually only about an hour from Albany, and the family had a mansion that wasn't being used about twenty minutes from where the party was, so the plan was for me to pick up Johnny from the Albany airport, drive down to the mansion, stay there that night, and go to the graduation party the next day.

 I picked up Johnny at 10 pm, pulling up at the baggage claim area just as he was walking out.

"Ready for an entertaining-as-fuck tour?" I asked him as he sat in the front seat.

"Hell yeah, man, let's do this. It should be lit," Johnny said, since us 30-somethings try to stay up to date with the younger crowd lingo (if you're not young and need some translation, lit basically means amazing).

Johnny admired my car. "I didn't know you had a BMW. Love the red interior."

"Thanks man. Yeah, I've been fortunate the past year."

"Looks that way!"

We started the one-hour drive southwest on I-88 from Albany. If you take 1-88 all the way, you wind up near Binghamton. If you only go halfway, you wind up literally nowhere. That was our destination.

Johnny Bananas and Andy with the ponies
before the graduation party appearance

It was a dark rainy night, and the fancy headlights on my Beamer were useless against the thick ominous fog. There were basically no other cars on the road. It felt like a scene from a horror movie.

It was near midnight when we got off the highway at the exact point of oblivion, following the GPS directions we were given. When I say there was nothing around us, believe me, there was Nothing. Johnny started getting nervous. "Are you sure this is a real gig? We might be being sent to our murders right now."

"They did send the deposit."

"Dude, we can't spend it if we're dead."

I tried to call the mom who booked the event, but there was no service. We proceeded down the country road slowly, but the GPS on my phone was going in and out. We could see about two feet in front of us in the fog. A pack of deer ran ahead of us. I hoped we were headed the right way. I had no idea. We could find the mansion, or we could end up in the Twilight Zone. It could go either way.

Five minutes later, there it was.

A sprawling, HUGE mansion. The lights were on, and there were a few people waiting outside for us. We weren't sure if this was a good sign or not.

"Say your prayers, Binder," Johnny said.

But it was the family and some friends of the girl graduating, and they were ecstatic to see us. We talked for a few, they got some pictures with Johnny, and we got a tour of the mansion we'd be staying in, all by ourselves.

It's hard to explain how surreal this place was. There were two full bars, with top shelf decades-old whisky that we were told was ours for the taking, a full gym, a sauna, a man cave with a pool table, old school arcade games like Pac-Man and Space Invaders, a vintage working juke box that played actual vinyl, a card table, a slot machine, and so on. Each bathroom had a heated toilet seat, as well as heated towel racks. And there was amazing rock n' roll memorabilia everywhere. Guitars and posters signed by rock legends. Including Elvis!

Where the hell were we?

Johnny and I spent the night alone in the mansion. There was no cell service (can't have everything!) but we played video games and the juke box for hours, drinking amazing whisky. He took the master suite, I took one of the spare bedrooms.

The next day we checked out our location in the cold light of day. The mansion was located on what looked like a hundred acres of farmland. About 30 feet from the house was a stable full of ponies, which sent Johnny into rapture. He loved ponies! (who knew?). He spent the rest of the morning hanging out at the stable with his new four-legged friends until I had to drag him away to the party.

We stopped at Wal-Mart on our way to pick up some props for the contests. Contests that would be a lot more appropriate for a high school graduation party than some of the wild ones we typically do in bars and nightclubs. Johnny would be hosting an Oreo-eating contest (you put the Oreo on your forehead and eat it without using your hands), a Kleenex contest (you pull the tissues out of the box one by one as fast as you can) and a non-alcoholic flip cup contest. The winning team would get a gold spray-painted banana as a prize. Johnny—always branding himself in every possible way.

When we showed up to the party I felt like we were still in an alternate universe. Shit, we didn't have high school graduation parties like this when I was younger. There were steamed clams, shrimp, and sushi, food trucks with unlimited wood-fired pizza, various high-end fry creations, an ice cream truck, and more. And there was an open top-shelf bar with several bartenders. Yeah, this was my kind of graduation party.

There were plenty of moms there, too, and they were not averse to the idea of partying with Johnny Bananas. It actually got a little out of hand. Some of the ladies got a little toasted, some got totally drunk, and it was these moms who ended up being the ones asking for non-stop pictures with Bananas. We ended up staying and partying for like six hours. But we called it an early night, because we had a lot of stops ahead of us and we didn't want to blow all of our energy the first day at a grad party.

So the tour went on.

We would be picking up some extra baggage for the next leg of our journey: Mario would obviously be joining us, as always wearing his black shirt labeled "Security." And this time my friend from Canada, Nolan, would be coming along for the ride as well. Nolan, who'd I actually met on a cruise and became good friends with, was a jacked firefighter from Toronto, and also one of the most polite and respectful guys I had known. And respect is so important to me. So when he made clear how he was dying to experience some of the craziness from a reality star tour, I absolutely invited him on board.

The plan was for both Mario and Nolan to meet us at our next stop: Hartford. Johnny was cool with it. Besides, he'd already known Mario for years and loved making fun of him.

"Mario still obsessed with bobos and hooking up with different girls at every event?" he wondered.

"It's all he talks about."

"Nice to see someone sticking to his principles."

We made great time to Hartford, and as I pulled into the

hotel front loop, my GPS announced, "You have arrived at your destination."

That's when Johnny looked up from his phone.

"What the FUCK?!" he shouted.

"What?" I asked.

"This is a Red Roof Inn!"

"Actually, it's a Red Roof Plus. Newly renovated."

"It's a Red Roof. There is NO FUCKING WAY I'm staying at a Red Roof!" he blasted.

"Dude, come on, really?"

"Yes, really! Find another hotel."

"This is what the bar booked for us—it's already paid for. I don't think we'll find one at this rate that you'll like any better."

"Find one if we're gonna stay in this city tonight!"

Ugh. Suddenly it all came back to me—the supreme aggravation of dealing with a Z-lister. Johnny may have been a friend, but he was still impressed with his own fame and not above pulling diva stunts. Pain in the ass!

Johnny Bananas on the bar pouring shots for fans at a gig

I called the bar manager and explained the situation as reasonably as possible: "Hey man, Johnny had a bad experience at a Red Roof in the past. I didn't know in advance or else I would've said something. Is there anything we can do to get a different hotel? Last time I did an event with you we were at the Homewood Suites down the road. Any chance you can hook us up there again?"

Andy and Johnny Bananas

"Well, It's gonna cost me more," the manager responded, "but we wanna take care of you guys and want you all happy, so I'll make it work,"

"Thanks, you're the best. Tonight is gonna be sick!" I promised.

I gave Johnny the good news. He seemed pleased. Well, he stopped whining so I figured he was pleased.

I texted Mario and Nolan the new hotel info, and we went over to the Homewood Suites to check in. My room was awesome. There was a living room and full kitchen, and a separate bedroom with a queen bed. Perfect—Mario and Nolan could sleep in the living room (Nolan could deal with the snoring—ha!), and I'd have my own private bedroom (and maybe some Hartford honey might join me?).

As I was lost in my happy thoughts, all of a sudden there was a loud banging on my door.

"Binder! Open up!" I heard Johnny yell.

I opened the door. "What's up, dude? Aren't these suites awesome?"

"No! I have a queen bed. We need to switch rooms," he demanded.

"What do you mean? I have a queen bed too," I said.

He walked into the suite bedroom to confirm that I was telling the truth.

"Fuck! Well, I have to change rooms. The bed is WAAAAYYY too small!"

"It's a queen bed, man! It's not tiny!" I said, in shock.

"I need a KING. You should know this. I'm going to the front desk."

And he walked out. He was sure acting Bananas, living up to his nickname. Was this the same laid-back mellow guy who just yesterday was frolicking with the ponies?

A few minutes later he texted me his new room number and I went over. It had a king bed, and a full living room and kitchen. So he was happy. Thank God.

Mario and Nolan arrived, we had some dinner, and then pre-gamed in my hotel suite before the appearance. Some things never changed. But the type of booze did. We had moved on from the Jäger years. It was all about Fireball Whiskey shots now. And we did several before heading over to the appearance.

The gig itself was typical insanity. Johnny got on the bar and poured shots in mouths, hosted some contests, and took pictures with hundreds of googly-eyed fans.

"Wow, you weren't kidding aboot how wild these appearances are, ey," my Canadian friend Nolan exclaimed.

"I remember my first time," said Mario. "Glad we got to break your reality star cherry." Mario then picked out our favorite female Banana fans and lifted them into the air over the crowd and set them on the bar to do body shots.

We invited them back to party at the hotel after. Nolan hooked up with his first reality-star groupie. Why not? He was Canadian,

AND associated with Johnny Bananas' crew. The ladies just couldn't resist.

And the tour went on.

We basically did a repeat of Hartford in Worcester, MA. The two-floor nightclub was hopping, the banana-flavored shots were pouring, and the girls were lining up for their chance to meet Johnny. And for the first time we experienced a custom Snapchat Geofilter for the event. The bar had ordered a Geo-filter with their name, logo, and Johnny Bananas's official logo. All of the hundreds of Snapchat users at the bar that night could tag all of their snaps with the Johnny Banana themed Geofilter. Branding again!

It really made me think how long I'd been doing this. When I first started I was taking fan pictures with disposable cameras. Then the fans would hand me digital cameras. Gradually smart-phones took over; and now I was being handed the phone with the Snapchat app already open. So many things had changed throughout the years. So many things hadn't.

And the tour went on.

The next stop was a day party in the resort town of Lake George, NY. If you've never been there, it's a beautiful spot—a pristine lake surrounded by green mountains in all directions. The village of Lake George is a hopping tourist destination during the summer months, and King Neptune's is the number one spot in town. They brought in Bananas to appear and host some contests during a day party event. The contests ranged from having to flip a cup onto a beer bottle, to shaking your body with an empty tissue box filled with ping pong balls tied around your waist to see who gets the most balls to fall out.

It was entertaining as fuck. And just another typical day on the Johnny Bananas Summer Tour.

And the tour went on.

We next headed down to Westerly, Rhode Island for an amazing beach party at a beach club down there. I had been there before with Wes, and I knew it would be a blast.

When we arrived we were brought right to the VIP cabana area. There were hundreds of girls in tiny bikinis dancing to the

DJ in the 90 degree heat of a sunny summer day. It was a beautiful scene.

So beautiful, in fact, that I ended up drinking just a little too much. Hey, come on, we were getting paid to be at New England's top beach club surrounded by sexy ladies. And the hot waitresses, in bikinis themselves, were handing out endless free drinks. How could I not partake?

We were at the party from 2 pm to 6 pm, and by the time it ended I had a girl giving me a lap dance in our cabana. I got her number and made plans to meet up with her later that night.

I remember getting back to the hotel at 6:30 pm. The plan was to change and then go back out. I'd meet up with my girl. Perfect.

The next thing I remember, I was looking at my phone and seeing the time say 6:35. I thought to myself, what the fuck? It was already 6:30 in the morning and the sun was coming out? I couldn't believe we had been out all night.

We hadn't. It was still 6:30 pm. Not realizing that, I passed out in our suite, and Mario and Nolan did the same.

Johnny tried to wake us up an hour later to go out. There was no response.

So he went out with the promoter himself, and had a good time from what I heard.

I was pissed off as fuck that I'd missed my chance to meet up with lap dance girl because I drank too much. I never saw her again.

Oh well. Shit happens. It was still a blast overall. The promoter got a kick out of it, and instead of being mad that we all drank too much and weren't necessarily as professional as we could've been, he actually liked us more for it. And assured me the next day he'd be calling me soon to book more events. Perfect!

And the tour went on.

Queens, New York City. If anything was going to go wrong on this tour, it would be here.

And it did.

I had doubts about this event from the start. But the routing—the distance between the previous tour stop and the next tour stop—fit, and we had the date open. So we decided to do it.

Johnny Bananas posing next to his event sign before heading into the Atlantic City appearance

This really sketchy promoter—even sketchier than Sid—was putting on a 90's theme party, and he wanted Johnny Bananas to host a karaoke contest. The problem was, the promoter was also a local rapper. And he was a lot more focused on his rap skills than in promoting. Johnny and the karaoke contest were supposed to be the opening act for this rapper.

WTF?!

Needless to say, this shit was not promoted at all, and NO ONE was there. OK, that's an exaggeration. About ten people showed up. That isn't an exaggeration. It was ridiculous.

If we hadn't gotten the deposit in advance, and if our hotel rooms weren't already pre-paid by Mr. Rapper, we wouldn't have showed. The venue itself was actually cool as fuck. It was a huge concert space. It could have held thousands. Instead, it was holding ten.

To make matters worse, the guy refused to pay us the rest of the money owed. and then left the building. They turned the air conditioning off, so it was a sauna in there. We took pictures with the ten fans, sang a few karaoke songs for the fun of it, and then peaced the fuck out of there.

I had of course learned that not everything can be perfect in the reality star tour world. Fortunately we all took it in stride, since the rest of the tour was going so well. In the past it could have been much, much worse. So, surprisingly, but thankfully, the stress was kept to a minimum.

And the tour went on.

We had one more stop on the Johnny Bananas Summer Tour. And it would end up being not only the best stop on the tour, but the best reality star gig I had ever done.

Atlantic City.

It started with the casino sending a limo to pick us up in New York City. Johnny loved being treated like an A-lister. "I'll bet friggin' Wes doesn't get a limo," he crowed.

It was a sausage-fest of a limo ride to AC, 2 hours with us guys just chilling in the limo. Would've been nice if some ladies were with us.

But it was still cool.

We were greeted at the hotel by a "talent VIP host", who handed us the keys to our suites. "Just text me if you want dinner reservations somewhere, we have comped $300 toward your dinner," she said. "We'll meet you at 12:30 am to walk you down to the club."

That's right, the gig was starting at 12:30 am. That's Atlantic City prime time.

Johnny was in a great mood. And he damn well should have been. He was treated like royalty, with a huge suite and a perfect king bed in it. No complaining from Mr. Diva for this gig.

Signs were all over the casino promoting the Johnny Bananas appearance at the nightclub that night. And everywhere we walked people ran up to us: "Ohmygod! Johnny Bananas! Can I have a pic?" asked girl after girl after girl.

Of course I was still on camera duty. Or to be specific, Snapchat duty.

We spent the next few hours relaxing and pregaming, and then we were walked down to the club. Our host and three security guards led us through the back hallways of the casino until we got right to the side entrance to the club.

Getting the official escort definitely made me feel, and know, that I was back on top.

And when we walked into Harrah's Pool After Dark, and DJ Hollywood, one of the best DJ's in existence, announced that Johnny Bananas was in the house, the thousands of people in the club went wild.

"What's up Atlantic City?!" Johnny shouted into the mic after Hollywood introduced him.

The crowd screamed.

"On the count of three, I want all of you to shout your favorite curse word!" Johnny ordered them. "One…Two…Three!"

The crowd all shouted at once. It was mostly "FUUUUUUUUC-CCKKKK!" Then they all cheered.

"I'm hanging out with you guys all night long! So come say hi!" Johnny said as he hopped off the stage, into the pit, to take pictures with fans.

I walked over to the VIP table and Mario handed me a drink.

"Can you believe we've been doing this for over a dozen years?" he asked.

"You mean *I've* been doing it. You've just been enjoying the perks," I replied loudly, over DJ Hollywood's amazing mix skills.

"Cheers to all the bobos, and more to come," Mario said.

"This is nuts. Thanks again for having me," the polite Canadian Nolan added in. I again appreciated his respect.

For over a dozen years. The ups and downs. The good and the bad. The successes and failures. And I was still here. I overcame the odds.

Jeff Timmons was the reason I didn't close up shop. Jeff and Men of the Strip pulled me out of my downward spiral and sent me skywards again.

Reality legends like Wes Bergmann and Johnny Bananas helped re-ignite the passion for working with reality stars that started me on my journey in the first place.

Z-List, A-List, and anywhere in between. I was still enjoying the ride.

Now Johnny came over to the table after mingling with his fans.

"Jameson and ginger for you," I said, handing him a drink.

"Sick gig, right, Binder?" he asked.

"Amazing gig," I responded.

"Cheers to Bananas!" Mario said.

"Cheers to Binder!" Bananas said.

"Cheers to all of us," I said as we all held up our drinks and cheered.

"Wouldn't this shit make a great reality show?" Bananas asked.

"Life on tour with reality stars. I like it!" I said.

Is that what would be next for us?

Who knew? Maybe.

But what I did know, is that I had no regrets. The past 12 years were a crazy rollercoaster ride, but I wouldn't have changed any of it.

CHAPTER 16

THE FUTURE OF Z

So where do we go from here?

To talk about the future of the Z-list seems like a contradiction in terms. By its nature, the Z-list connotes ordinariness, mediocrity, a lack of talent, a celebrity without merit. There's no future there. Anyone who makes it to the Z-list has already hit his or her peak, and it should be all downhill from here.

I know that's how I felt, I'm not gonna lie. There was a time when I thought the Z-future was non-existent. I was so annoyed, pissed, and angry at my own prospects that I was about to close up shop. My only expectation for the future was no gigs, no money, and shitty jobs. All these glorified reality icons would likely wind up as the next Hooters girl or a server at Applebee's.

But I was wrong. So wrong. And once I turned the page and was able to expand my client list, I was able to see things clearer. A rising tide lifts all boats. That much-reviled *Jersey Shore* powerhouse that we all lamented for its oxygen-sucking monopoly actually ended up increasing demand and bookings for all reality stars. Which has led to new hit shows popping up and more and more clients. New shows like MTV's Siesta Key are as popular as they are today because of their predesessors. And a recent event I did, with hundreds of fans screaming in delight waiting to meet the Siesta Key reality stars I booked, proves even more that the Z-List is here to stay. Because of the popularity of all of these shows, the reality fan base has kept growing, and growing, and growing. And now millions of fans, young and old, of all backgrounds, continue to be obsessed with reality TV personalities. They feel a genuine personal connection to them. Some fans even feel like they're in love with them.

Of course it's all an illusion. They don't really know anything about their idols' personal lives, their goals, their dreams. But still, I'm happy the fans are obsessed or in love. It's why we keep getting the tours, the money, and those endless insane, crazy experiences.

But what about those real dreams of the Z-listers? Do they all want to be on TV forever? Do they all want to keep doing these wild, ridiculous appearances, as entertaining and lucrative as they may be?

Some, yes. Others, no.

The taste of Z-list stardom has led many to hope for A-list fame. This may be a farfetched notion for some, but for an anointed few, there is a brighter future in show biz.

Looking back, many original Z-list reality stars from before my time went on to become very successful actors and celebrities.

Think WWE star Mike 'The Miz' Mizanin, who originally starred in MTV's *Real World: Back to New York* and is now a WWE superstar.

Think David Giuntoli, who originally starred in MTV's *Road Rules South Pacific*, and is now a very successful actor, who most notably had the starring role in NBC's hit show *Grimm*.

Think Jamie Chung, who originally starred in MTV's *Real World: San Diego* and has gone on to become a successful television actress, starring in such shows as NBC's *Believe* and FOX's *Gotham*.

Think Jacinda Barrett, who originally starred in MTV's *Real World: London*; she has also gone on to become a very successful actress, appearing in many movies including *Poseidon* and *School for*

Scoundrels, as well as starring in several TV series including NBC's *Zero Hour* and Netflix's *Bloodline*.

Damn! Those are some big jumps on the celebrity letter list for a lucky few MTV reality star alums.

So maybe it's a long shot for some newer Z-listers who harbor the same dream. But it's definitely not an impossibility.

Take Johnny Bananas. He's been on every season of MTV's *The Challenge* since he first appeared on *Real World: Key West* in 2005. He's made a living appearing on the shows, winning the competitions, and doing gigs and events around the country. And he turned that into his own brand, selling high quality Johnny Bananas themed t-shirts, sweatshirts and hats. Every single gig I do with him there's at least several fans that come up to Johnny wearing his branded apparel. And Johnny keeps getting bigger and bigger. Allow me to remind you that you can order your own Bananas gear at his website realjohnny-bananas.com.

All of this exposure is part of Johnny's game plan for the future. One of his most famous fans, the legendary Jimmy Fallon, recently even had him as one of his Tonight Show guests! His next goal is hosting his own TV show. Given his success thus far, I can easily see him pulling it off.

But not all reality stars dream of making the A-list. In fact, many of them use the money they earned from TV winnings and appearances to further their very practical business aspirations.

Mr. Beautiful, Kenny Santucci, now is part owner of a successful fitness training business in New York City: Solace. It makes sense: he knows how to stay beautiful if anyone does. You can find out more about it, and even hire him as your own personal trainer, at kenny-santucci.com.

Evan Starkman runs The Bait Shoppe, a full service experiential marketing agency. If you want some creative ways to market your brand, check out what he does at baitshoppe.com.

Perhaps the best case for using the Z-list as a launching pad is made by my good friend, the legendary world-famous ginger, Wes Bergmann.

Wes has always been a good businessman. He can sell any idea to anyone. He sure as hell has sold me on a lot of ideas throughout the years.

Wes used his business knowledge to create Betablox, a business incubator. He gets applications and pitches from hundreds of start-up businesses in Kansas City and Tulsa each year, and selects the top several dozen. The ones selected get to be "incubated" through Betablox. Wes and his team provide the office space, resources, professional mentors, industry connections and more to help bring these start-ups to superstar business status. In return, Wes owns 5% equity in every one. So, in effect, Wes owns part of hundreds and hundreds of businesses.

All while appearing on almost every season of *The Challenge*. His appearance fees and Challenge winnings serve as the endless funding source for his incubator. Betablox would not be the huge success that it is if not for Wes' original Z-list fame and cash flow (if you're starting up a unique new business in the Tulsa or Kansas City area that you think could use the resources and guidance that a business incubator can provide, check out betablox.com to see application guidelines).

So props to Wes. He did it right. So did Evan and Kenny and so many others. They used their Z-list fame to launch their business careers. And their future is bright.

As it is for many reality stars who have gone on to participate in the actual real world, and get real world jobs. Former Z-listers are now doctors, lawyers, nurses, EMTs, authors, politicians, you name it.

Their Z-list days were only one part of their life experience. It was a part almost none would ever have given up.

And up-and-coming Z-listers know this. They see the fame and money that the reality stars have gotten, and want a piece of it. New reality shows are popping up every single season on every single network.

But you don't need to be cast on a reality show to make it to the Z-list. Start up your own YouTube channel and do something creative to get thousands of subscribers. Make a really unique Instagram page and become social media Z-list famous.

There are so many ways to make it work. And because of that, the Z-list is not going anywhere. Not by a long shot.

Reality TV fame can mean many things:

It can be a stepping stone to celebrity A-list stardom.

It can be a revenue generator, a path to business success.

It can be just another notch on the resume in the career path to something else.

Or it can be a way of life.

For me, it was all of the above.

It was a stepping stone to working with bigger celebrities. It generated money to invest back into my business. It gave me experience and made me more in demand by colleges, theaters, nightclubs and other venues and promoters looking to work with a real professional. And, of course, it's been a way of life for me ever since I first met Veronica and Rachel so many years ago.

I couldn't imagine my life without the Z-listers. I feel lucky for all I've experienced with them, and honored and proud to be included in their world. And it sure as hell is a lot bigger world than you could ever have imagined just by watching their shows.

So no, I don't see an end to the Z-list in my future. I see it growing. Sure, I'll represent bigger celebrities. I'll work with colleges and large venues to bring in the big shows, and my client list will expand. But, through it all, reality TV stars will always be a part of my world.

And as I stand in a sold-out theater, listening to the thousands of fans scream in delight, I can't help but reflect on how the last 14 years have been a rollercoaster of surprises, fun, drama, shock, stupor, and endless variety: the spice of life.

Andy, Angelina, Jeff and Mario all hanging out in Atlantic City

ACKNOWLEDGEMENTS

ALL OF MY ADVENTURES THAT YOU'VE just experienced wouldn't have been possible without the support, guidance, and assistance from so many people.

I first have to thank my parents, Mike and Nancy. Although I know they probably didn't like reading some parts of this book, throughout my life they have supported me and whatever path I took, despite the fact that it definitely has not been a normal path.

I'd also like to thank my brother Jon, the rational one of the family. His opinions help me see things from a completely different perspective. Usually the opposite of my own.

Of course a special thank you goes out to several reality stars who have been integral in my life; to Veronica and Rachel for originally teaching me how the reality star booking business works; to Wes, my closest reality star friend, who I look to for continual guidance on business savvy decisions; to Dunbar for being so supportive and excited when telling him about this book; to Johnny Bananas for always keeping me on my toes and keeping the demand for reality star events higher than ever; and to every other reality star who was mentioned in this book and has been a part of this crazy ride. Thank you.

I huge thank you to legendary security guard/ driver/ bobo lover Mario Nacev. The number of times he's assisted with getting reality stars to gigs, helped defuse out of hand situations at events, tipped the bartenders $100 when the rest of us forgot to, and entertained us with his one of a kind personality is countless. Thanks dude.

Another big thank you to Jeff Timmons for believing in my drive and passion and bringing me into the Men of the Strip team; and to Jeff's wife Amanda for always making sure I know who the real boss is.

Thanks to my friends Gavin, Mayo, Justin, Hunter, and Nolan for being a part of these adventures and adding to the insanity.

I am also grateful to all of the nightclubs, bars, colleges and other venues that have brought us in for events and appearances throughout the years. This book wouldn't have existed without them.

A special thank you also goes out to my good friend Josh, an English professor whose expertise I relied on with many questions throughout the writing of this book.

And speaking of writing, another major thank you to Fred Stroppel for helping me turn my story into words that flow page after page.

I also have to give a shout out to my amazing Boston Terrier, Chase, for keeping me company while I wrote.

And a thank you goes out to Ceara Poulin for taking an extremely entertaining cover photo, and helping to get it all together on such short notice. And thanks to Harley, Anna, Danielle, Felicia, Jillian, Courtney, Mackenzie, Kristin, Natasha and Taylor. You all made great cover models. Also, thank you to Lee Dixon for bringing that cover together with an excellent design.

Last, but definitely not least, a big thank you to everyone at Blue River Press and Cardinal Publishers Group for making *Harsh Reality* a reality. Especially to Tom Doherty for believing in the project, and to my editor Dani McCormick for her guidance, suggestions, hard work, and constant communication throughout the entire process. Thank you so much.

APPENDIX: REALITY STARS AND SHOWS*

All reality stars mentioned in *Harsh Reality*

and the reality shows they participated in

all shows appeared on MTV unless otherwise noted

Angelina Pivarnick
The Jersey Shore (2009-2010)
Couples Therapy (2012) – on VH1

Caitlin Ryder
Select episodes of The Jersey Shore (2009-2012)

Cohutta Grindstaff
Real World: Sydney (2007)
The Challenge: The Island (2008)
The Challenge: The Ruins (2009)
The Challenge: Free Agents (2014)
The Challenge: Battle of the Bloodlines (2015)

Deena Cortese
The Jersey Shore (2010-2012)
Couples Therapy (2014) – on VH1

Dunbar Merrill
Real World: Sydney (2007)
The Challenge: The Island (2008)
The Challenge: The Duel 2 (2009)
The Challenge: The Ruins (2009)
The Challenge: Cutthroat (2010)
The Challenge: Battle of the Exes (2012)
The Challenge: Rivals 2 (2013)

Evan Starkman
The Challenge: Fresh Meat (2006)
The Challenge: The Duel (2006)
The Challenge: The Gauntlet 3 (2008)
The Challenge: The Duel 2 (2009)
The Challenge: The Ruins (2009)
Spring Break Challenge (2010)
The Challenge: Rivals (2011)
Love Trap (2011) – Host on Cosmo TV Canada

Isaac Stout
Real World: Sydney (2007)
The Challenge: The Duel 2 (2009)
The Challenge: Free Agents (2014)

Johanna Botta
Real World: Austin (2005)
The Challenge: Fresh Meat (2006)
The Challenge: The Gauntlet 3 (2008)
The Challenge: The Island (2008)
The Challenge: The Ruins (2009)

Johnny Bananas
Real World: Key West (2006)

The Challenge: The Duel (2006)
The Challenge: The Inferno 3 (2007)
The Challenge: The Gauntlet 3 (2008)
The Challenge: The Island (2008)
The Challenge: The Ruins (2009)
The Challenge: Cutthroat (2010)
The Challenge: Rivals (2011)
The Challenge: Battle of the Exes (2012)
The Challenge: Rivals 2 (2013)
The Challenge: Free Agents (2014)
The Challenge: Battle of the Exes 2 (2015)
The Challenge: Battle of the Bloodlines (2015)
The Challenge: Rivals 3 (2016)
The Challenge: Invasion of the Champions (2017)
The Challenge: Champs vs. Pros (2017)
The Challenge: Dirty 30 (2017)
The Challenge: Champs vs. Stars (2017)
The Challenge: Vendettas (2018)

Kenny Santucci
The Challenge: Fresh Meat (2006)
The Challenge: The Duel (2006)
The Challenge: The Inferno 3 (2007)
The Challenge: The Gauntlet 3 (2008)
The Challenge: The Island (2008)
The Challenge: The Ruins (2009)
The Challenge: Fresh Meat 2 (2010)
Spring Break Challenge (2010)
The Challenge: Rivals (2011)

Landon Lueck
Real World: Philadelphia (2004)
The Challenge: The Inferno 2 (2005)
The Challenge: The Gauntlet 2 (2005)
The Challenge: The Duel 2 (2009)
The Challenge: Fresh Meat 2 (2010)
Spring Break Challenge (2010)

Nehemiah Clark
Real World: Austin (2005)
The Challenge: The Duel (2006)
The Challenge: The Gauntlet 3 (2008)
The Challenge: The Duel 2 (2009)
The Challenge: Rivals (2011)

Nicole "Snooki" Polizzi
The Jersey Shore (2009-2012)
Snooki and Jwow (2012-2014)
Snooki and Jionni's Shore Flip (2016) – on FIY Network
The Celebrity Apprentice (2017) – on NBC
Celebrity Shore (2018) – on VH1

Parisa Montazaran
Real World Sydney (2007)

Paula Meronak
Real World Key West (2006)
The Challenge: The Duel (2006)
The Challenge: The Inferno 3 (2007)
The Challenge: The Gauntlet 3 (2008)
The Challenge: The Island (2008)
The Challenge: The Duel 2 (2009)
The Challenge: Fresh Meat 2 (2010)
Spring Break Challenge (2010)
The Challenge: Cutthroat (2010)
The Challenge: Rivals (2011)
The Challenge: Battle of the Exes (2012)
The Challenge: Rivals 2 (2013)

Rachel Robinson
Road Rules: Campus Crawl (2002)
The Challenge: Battle of the Sexes (2003)
The Challenge: The Gauntlet (2003)
The Challenge: Battle of the Sexes 2 (2004)
The Challenge: The Inferno 2 (2005)

The Challenge: The Island (2008)
The Challenge: The Duel 2 (2009)
The Challenge: Battle of the Exes (2012)

Shane Landrum
Road Rules: Campus Crawl (2002)
The Challenge: Battle of the Sexes (2003)
The Challenge: The Inferno (2004)
The Challenge: Battle of the Sexes (2004)
The Challenge: Fresh Meat (2006)
The Challenge: Invasion of the Champions (2017)
The Challenge: Vendettas (2018)

Shauvon Torres
Real World: Sydney (2007)
The Challenge: The Duel 2 (2009)
The Challenge: The Ruins (2009)
The Challenge: Cutthroat (2010)

Trisha Cummings
Real World Sydney (2007)

Veronica Portillo
Road Rules: Semester at Sea (1999)
Challenge 2000 (2000)
The Challenge: Battle of the Seasons (2002)
The Challenge: Battle of the Sexes (2003)
The Challenge: The Gauntlet (2003)
The Challenge: The Inferno (2004)
The Challenge: Battle of the Sexes 2 (2004)
The Challenge: The Inferno 2 (2005)
The Challenge: The Ruins (2009)
The Challenge: Dirty 30 (2017)
The Challenge: Champs vs Pros (2017)
The Challenge: Vendettas (2018)

Wes Bergmann
Real World: Austin (2005)
The Challenge: Fresh Meat (2006)
The Challenge: The Duel (2006)
The Challenge: The Ruins (2009)
The Challenge: Fresh Meat 2 (2010)
Spring Break Challenge (2010)
The Challenge: Rivals (2011)
The Challenge: Battle of the Exes (2012)
The Challenge: Battle of the Seasons (2012)
The Challenge: Rivals 2 (2013)
The Challenge: Battle of the Exes 2 (2015)
The Challenge: Rivals 3 (2016)
The Challenge: Champs vs. Pros (2017)
The Challenge: Champs vs. Stars (2017)

ABOUT THE AUTHOR

ANDY BINDER GREW UP IN CLIFTON Park, NY and earned his Bachelor's Degree from the State University of New York at Geneseo and his Master's Degree from The College of Saint Rose. For over a dozen years he has spent much of his time operating his talent agency, Tobinder Talent Booking, booking reality stars, and more recently several singers and other acts all over the United States and Canada. When not booking events or traveling to appearances and shows with his clients, Andy likes spending his free time on his boat in Lake George, NY, going to concerts, cruising to exotic locations, having drinks with friends, meeting new people, and spending time with his local family including his parents, brother, sister-in-law, and two nieces. He currently resides in Albany, NY with his Boston Terrier, Chase.

To find out more information on acts that Andy is currently representing, including details for booking opportunities for Men of the Strip, Jeff Timmons, and reality stars Johnny Bananas and Wes Bergmann and more, check out Tobinder Talent Booking, LLC's website at www.tobinder.com. For any specific questions or comments, Andy can be reached directly at andy@tobinder.com.